Murray Walker's
GRAND PRIX YEAR

Foreword by
FRANK WILLIAMS

Photography
JOHN TOWNSEND

PUBLISHED IN ASSOCIATION WITH ICI

ACKNOWLEDGEMENTS

To me the Grand Prix year is a non-stop happening full of excitement, drama, colour and achievement. I have always wanted to record one and now I've done it. I don't suppose I would ever have got around to it if it hadn't been for Roger Chown, who not only bravely made this his first publishing venture, but who also originated the idea and was my guide and mentor throughout its development.

In doing the actual thinking and writing I have found, as I am sure every author has, that it wouldn't have been possible without a great deal of help from a lot of fine people. My many friends in the pit lane — the Drivers, Team Owners, Managers, Sponsors, Mechanics, Trade Representatives and PR people. My friends in that cheerful band of knowledgeable experts the Grand Prix journalists. In particular Nigel Roebuck of *Autosport*, Alan Henry of *Motoring News*, Maurice Hamilton of *Autocourse*, Eoin Young of *Autocar* and Mike Doodson and Jeff Hutchinson of virtually everything else.

But I wouldn't even have been there if it hadn't been for the support and encouragement I've always had from my masters at the BBC. Jonathan Martin who first knocked me into shape. Roger Moody under whose ebullient leadership the *Grand Prix* programme consolidated its great success. And Charles Balchin who has more than maintained its very high standards.

My deep appreciation and grateful thanks to each and every one of them and also to two other special people. Frank Williams who managed to find the time in his demanding and pressurised life to write the foreword — which I deeply appreciate. And Geoff Wootton who has done such an excellent job in designing a book which superbly reflects the spirit and feeling of the Grand Prix world that means so much to me.

Lastly, although she should really have been first, my wife Elizabeth, who keeps my complicated life afloat and uncomplainingly accepts me constantly disappearing instead of mowing the grass.

I've enjoyed writing this book as much as I enjoy being a part of the Grand Prix scene. I hope you enjoy reading it.

Murray Walker

Publisher's note

The publishers would like to acknowledge the help given by *The Marlboro Grand Prix Guide*, Steven Tee (for his picture on page 74), All-Sport (for their picture on page 86/87), Stuart Sykes and Ann Bradshaw, Jane Goddard, John Hayward, Peter Windsor, Martin Whitaker, H. W. Grimwade, Steve Hallam, Hugh Hastings, Gill Perkins, our friends at ICI, and finally Peter and Jane Gurr and Team Lotus in whose hospitality motor home the idea for this book was nourished.

Published by Clifford Frost Publications
and First Formula Publishing
In association with
First published 1987
© Murray Walker 1987
ISBN 1 870066 04 9

Edited by Roger Chown. Designed by Geoff Wootton.
Typeset, printed and produced by
Clifford Frost Ltd, Lyon Road, Wimbledon SW19 2SE.
Colour reproduction by Sinclair Graphics.

CONTENTS

FORMULA ONE GRAND PRIX RACE STATISTICS TO 1986

DRIVERS' WORLD CHAMPIONSHIP

1950 Giuseppe Farina, ITA (Alfa Romeo)
1951 Juan-Manuel Fangio, ARG (Alfa Romeo)
1952 Alberto Ascari, ITA (Ferrari)
1953 Alberto Ascari, ITA (Ferrari)
1954 Juan-Manuel Fangio, ARG (Maserati/Mercedes)
1955 Juan-Manuel Fangio, ARG (Mercedes)
1956 Juan-Manuel Fangio, ARG (Lancia/Ferrari)
1957 Juan-Manuel Fangio, ARG (Maserati)
1958 Mike Hawthorn, GB (Ferrari)
1959 Jack Brabham, AUS (Cooper-Climax)
1960 Jack Brabham, AUS (Cooper-Climax)
1961 Phil Hill, USA (Ferrari)
1962 Graham Hill, GB (BRM)
1963 Jim Clark, GB (Lotus-Climax)
1964 John Surtees, GB (Ferrari)
1965 Jim Clark, GB (Lotus-Climax)
1966 Jack Brabham, AUS (Brabham-Repco)
1967 Denis Hulme, NZ (Brabham-Repco)
1968 Graham Hill, GB (Lotus-Ford)
1969 Jackie Stewart, GB (Matra-Ford)
1970 Jochen Rindt, AUT (Lotus-Ford)
1971 Jackie Stewart, GB (Tyrrell-Ford)
1972 Emerson Fittipaldi, BRA (Lotus-Ford)
1973 Jackie Stewart, GB (Tyrrell-Ford)
1974 Emerson Fittipaldi, BRA (McLaren-Ford)
1975 Niki Lauda, AUT (Ferrari)
1976 James Hunt, GB (McLaren-Ford)
1977 Niki Lauda, AUT (Ferrari)
1978 Mario Andretti, USA (Lotus-Ford)
1979 Jody Scheckter, SA (Ferrari)
1980 Alan Jones, AUS (Williams-Ford)
1981 Nelson Piquet, BRA (Brabham-Ford)
1982 Keke Rosberg, FIN (Williams-Ford)
1983 Nelson Piquet, BRA (Brabham-BMW)
1984 Niki Lauda, AUT (McLaren-TAG/Porsche)
1985 Alain Prost, FRA (McLaren-TAG/Porsche)
1986 Alain Prost, FRA (McLaren-TAG/Porsche)

CONSTRUCTORS' WORLD CHAMPIONSHIP

1958 Vanwall
1959 Cooper
1960 Cooper
1961 Ferrari
1962 BRM
1963 Lotus
1964 Ferrari
1965 Lotus
1966 Brabham
1967 Brabham
1968 Lotus
1969 Matra
1970 Lotus
1971 Tyrrell
1972 Lotus
1973 Lotus
1974 McLaren
1975 Ferrari
1976 Ferrari
1977 Ferrari
1978 Lotus
1979 Ferrari
1980 Williams
1981 Williams
1982 Ferrari
1983 Ferrari
1984 McLaren
1985 McLaren
1986 Williams

GP WINS

		RACES CONTESTED
27	Jackie Stewart	99
25	Jim Clark	72
25	Niki Lauda	171
25	Alain Prost	105
24	Juan-Manuel Fangio	51
17	Nelson Piquet	126
16	Stirling Moss	66
14	Jack Brabham	126
14	Emerson Fittipaldi	144
14	Graham Hill	176
13	Alberto Ascari	32
12	Mario Andretti	128
12	Alan Jones	116
12	Carlos Reuteman	146
10	James Hunt	92
10	Ronnie Peterson	123
10	Jody Scheckter	112

Others

7	René Arnoux	112
7	Nigel Mansell	90
5	Michele Albereto	89
4	Ayrton Senna	46
2	Riccardo Patrese	144
1	Gerhard Berger	36

POLE POSITIONS

33	Jim Clark
28	Juan-Manuel Fangio
24	Niki Lauda
20	Nelson Piquet
18	Mario Andretti
18	René Arnoux
17	Jackie Stewart
16	Stirling Moss
16	Alain Prost
15	Ayrton Senna
14	James Hunt
14	Ronnie Peterson
13	Jack Brabham
13	Graham Hill
13	Jacky Ickx
10	Jochen Rindt

Others

4	Nigel Mansell
3	Teo Fabi
2	Michele Alboreto
2	Riccardo Patrese
1	Andrea De Cesaris

FASTEST LAPS

27	Jim Clark
25	Niki Lauda
23	Juan-Manuel Fangio
20	Stirling Moss
19	Nelson Piquet
18	Alain Prost
15	Clay Regazzoni
15	Jackie Stewart
14	Jacky Ickx
13	Alan Jones
12	René Arnoux
11	Alberto Ascari
11	John Surtees
10	Mario Andretti
10	Jack Brabham
10	Graham Hill

Others

6	Nigel Mansell
4	Ayrton Senna
3	Michele Alboreto
3	Riccardo Patrese
2	Gerhard Berger
2	Derek Warwick
1	Andrea De Cesaris
1	Teo Fabi

FOREWORD

If you, like me, have always wondered what it would be like to listen to Murray Walker with the sound turned down, then read on: here is the book for which we have been waiting. *Murray Walker's Grand Prix Year* provides a view from the television commentary chair — from a seat that Murray has occupied with tremendous success and enthusiasm for the past decade.

Television has become an integral part of Grand Prix racing. We work in a multi-million pound business over several continents for ten intensive months of the year. Murray's work with the BBC has become a part of that business in a way that is both irreplaceable and, dare I say, unique. It was not until I was confined to bed following a road accident in 1986 that I began to watch Grands Prix on television for any length of time. Very quickly I became a fan — not only of racing as seen on the box but also of the job that Murray is doing. It is very difficult to understand the machinations and nuances of a Grand Prix as it unfolds in front of you. Doing so from a stuffy commentary box remote from the action is harder still — and Murray is a master of the art.

We have here a concise yet readable account of the 1987 season as seen through the eyes of Murray Walker. The essential information is there, together with the sort of insight that only a man in Murray's position can provide. From his metaphorical position on top of the sport, Murray has seen and heard just about everything that goes on in Grand Prix racing. It is here, in easy-to-read form.

I am delighted to have the opportunity to welcome you to *Murray Walker's Grand Prix Year*. 1987 was for the Canon Williams-Honda team a year to remember — and I can think of nothing more fitting than for it to have been encapsulated in written form by Murray. The sound of his voice will be with us forever; to enjoy this book, though, you need neither a television nor a video. I hope you enjoy it as much as I have.

FRANK WILLIAMS

Michele Alboreto   Philippe Alliot   René Arnoux   Gerhard Berger

1987 DRIVERS PICTURE GALLERY

Ivan Capelli   Eddie Cheever   Yannick Dalmas

Franco Forini   Piercarlo Ghinzani   Stefan Johansson   Nicola Larini

Jonathan Palmer   Riccardo Patrese   Nelson Piquet   Alain Prost

Thierry Boutsen   Martin Brundle   Alex Caffi   Adrian Campos

Christian Danner   Andrea De Cesaris   Teo Fabi   Pascal Fabre

Nigel Mansell   Roberto Moreno   Satoru Nakajima   Alessandro Nannini

Ayrton Senna   Philippe Streiff   Gabriele Tarquini   Derek Warwick

No	Name	Nationality	Age	No. GP's	No Victories	Teams	Cars
1.	Alain Prost	FRA	32	105	25	Marlboro McLaren-TAG	MP4/3
2.	Stefan Johansson	SWE	30	44	—	Marlboro McLaren-TAG	MP4/3
3.	Jonathan Palmer	GBR	30	39	—	Data General Tyrrell-Ford	DG/016
4.	Philippe Streiff	FRA	31	22	—	Data General Tyrrell-Ford	DG/016
5.	Nigel Mansell	GBR	32	90	7	Canon Williams-Honda	FW11B
6.	Nelson Piquet	BRA	34	126	17	Canon Williams-Honda	FW11B
7.	Riccardo Patrese	ITA	33	144	2	MRD Brabham-BMW	BT56
8.	Andrea De Cesaris	ITA	27	88	—	MRD Brabham-BMW	BT56
9.	Martin Brundle	GBR	27	38	—	West Zakspeed	861
10.	Christian Danner	GER	29	17	—	West Zakspeed	861
11.	Satoru Nakajima	JAP	34	—	—	Camel Lotus-Honda	99T
12.	Ayrton Senna	BRA	27	46	4	Camel Lotus-Honda	99T
14.	Pascal Fabre	FRA	27	—	—	El Charro AGS-Ford	JH22
16.	Ivan Capelli	ITA	23	4	—	Leyton House March-Ford	RT 879
17.	Derek Warwick	GBR	32	68	—	USF & G Arrows-Megatron	A10
18.	Eddie Cheever	USA	29	86	—	USF & G Arrows-Megatron	A10
19.	Teo Fabi	ITA	32	48	—	Benetton-Ford	B187
20.	Thierry Boutsen	BEL	29	57	—	Benetton-Ford	B187
21.	Alex Caffi	ITA	23	1	—	Osella-Alfa Romeo	FA 11
23.	Adrian Campos	SPA	26	—	—	Minardi-Motori Moderni	M186
24.	Alessandro Nannini	ITA	27	15	—.	Minardi-Motori Moderni	M186
25.	Rene Arnoux	FRA	38	112	7	Gitanes Ligier-Megatron*	JS 29B
26.	Piercarlo Ghinzani	ITA	35	51	—	Gitanes Ligier-Megatron*	JS 29B
27.	Michele Alboreto	ITA	30	89	5	Ferrari	F 187
28.	Gerhard Berger	AUS	27	36	1	Ferrari	F 187
30.	Philippe Alliot	FRA	32	33	—	Larousse Calmels Lola-Ford	LC87

The Gitanes-Ligier team were originally scheduled to compete in the '87 season with Alfa Romeo engines. Following a disagreement with Alfa, Ligier missed the first race, and began their campaign at San Marino with Megatron engines.

APPENDIX
During the course of the 1987 season, Gabriele Tarquini (ITA) and Franco Forini (SUI) made their F1 debuts, both driving for Osella, as did Nicola Larini (ITA) driving for Coloni. Yannick Dalmas (FRA) started his Grand Prix career driving for Lola, and Roberto Moreno (BRA) too, was a GP debutant in the AGS, as was Stefano Modena (ITA) in the Brabham.

PREFACE

ONE of the most fascinating things about the superb car-and-driver spectacle we call Grand Prix Racing is the fact that, year by year, it is an ever-changing scene — different rules, different cars, different drivers, different circuits, different sponsors. A kaleidoscopic cocktail of speed, noise, colour, people, politics and excitement that makes a truly heady mix.

The 1986 season, no exception, made a superb prelude to 1987.

For the first time since Renault innovatively introduced 1½ litre turbocharged engines to Grand Prix racing in 1977 every car in every race was powered by a 'turbo'. The superb three-litre Ford-Cosworth DFV with its glorious V8 sound had run its last Grand Prix after a record 155 victories — we thought! For little did we realise at the beginning of the season that it would be back, bigger and better, in 1987.

As the tight little world of Grand Prix insiders — the teams, their sponsors, suppliers and the media people who move around the world together — looked forward to 1986 they did so with the knowledge that, for mainly financial reasons, the long-standing Dutch and South African races had been dropped from the sixteen race calendar. Instead we would be going to Hungary — the first time a World Championship Grand Prix had been held in a Communist bloc country — and back to Mexico which had last held an absolutely chaotic event in 1970. Both events turned out to be tremendously successful.

1986 was the story of three teams and four drivers; Williams, McLaren and Lotus. Alain Prost, Nelson Piquet, Nigel Mansell and Ayrton Senna. Between them, with one exception, they won every race, with Prost taking the Drivers' Championship and Williams the Constructors' Championship.

I think it is fair to say that, until 1986, most people regarded Nigel Mansell as an extremely good, tough and courageous driver who could win races but never the World Championship. How wrong he proved them to be! In his Williams-Honda, clearly the car of the year (it won nine of the sixteen races and the Constructors' Championship), Mansell won more races than anyone else and, with new found maturity, led the Drivers' Championship from mid-season right up to the last race in Australia. There the man who is freely acknowledged to be the most complete Grand Prix driver of them all (and one of the greatest

of all time), Frenchman Alain Prost, snatched the title from Mansell with a brilliant victory after having been the most consistent driver of the year. His, moreover, was the first 'two in a row' Championship win since that of Sir Jack Brabham in 1960.

So two of 1986's top men were Europeans. The other two were Brazilian. Nelson Piquet,

John Barnard — would he be able to put Maranello back on top?

already a double World Champion, did not win the title partly because his partner in the dominant Williams-Honda team was Mansell. Piquet, like Prost, won four times — one less than Mansell — but although his countryman Ayrton Senna won 'only' twice in his Lotus-Renault he proved that his is a very rare talent

The man they trust with their lives — FISA medical consultant Professor Sid Watkins — the most respected man in Grand Prix racing.

for he also achieved an incredible eight pole positions — a 50% success rate!

But if 1986 had its high points it also had some tragic lows. The sad death of the gentlemanly and personable Elio de Angelis in a testing crash at the Paul Ricard circuit. The terrible road crash which has confined the tremendously popular Williams team boss, Frank Williams, to a wheelchair for the rest of his life. The rally crash which forced the retirement of Marc Surer and the British Grand Prix first corner disaster which finished the Formula One career of the ever-popular Jacques Laffite. In these days of greatly improved safety precautions Motor Sport may be less hazardous than it was but it can still be very cruel indeed to its devotees.

1986 may have seen some changes but 1987 saw an absolute upheaval! New formula, new cars, new engines. The Canadian Grand Prix out. The Japanese Grand Prix in. No less than sixteen of the twenty-six drivers registered for the first Grand Prix, in Brazil, were either new to Formula One or with new teams. Dramatic designer defections. Only one tyre supplier. A much-changed and very intriguing scene.

Mid-way through the 1986 season the

Support for Grand Prix racing is always welcome!

Patrick Head — built like a tank, thinks like a genius, designs winners for Williams.

governing body of Motor Sport, FISA, decreed that the turbocars, which were then producing over 1,300 qualifying horsepower from their 1½ litre engines, had got to be phased out — 'too fast and too dangerous' they said. So, for 1987, their maximum permissible boost pressure would be reduced. Non-turbo cars, 3½ litres, with a lower weight, would be allowed to compete against the turbos and the category would have its own special awards. For the Constructors the Colin Chapman Trophy and, for the Drivers, the Jim Clark Trophy awarded, respectively, in memory of the great founder of Lotus and the Team's most successful driver. In 1988 the turbos would be further penalised and in 1989 they would be outlawed altogether.

The changed circumstances for 1987 were expected to make little difference. The turbocars would be affected only in qualifying. In the races they would still produce nearly 50% more power than their 3½ litre normally-aspirated rivals although the lighter weight of the bigger-engined cars was expected to help them be more competitive in the 'City Streets' races like Monaco and Detroit. Time would tell — and it did!

Would 1987 be kind to Derek Warwick?

Second in 1986 — Head man in '87?

*'No I can't afford it Alain!' McLaren mastermind
Ron Dennis talks business with his No. 1.*

joined the ailing Ferrari team. From Brabham the equally outstanding Gordon Murray switched to McLaren. With the total withdrawal of Renault from Grands Prix the three teams they had supplied with engines had to find their power somewhere else. Lotus pulled a master-stroke by persuading Honda to supply them as well as Williams. Honda did so on condition that Japanese driver Satoru Nakajima replaced Johnny Dumfries. Ligier's coup was to get Alfa-Romeo to design, produce and supply them exclusively with a new turbo engine. But the deal foundered when Ligier's outspoken driver, Rene Arnoux, publicly condemned the Alfa engine. Exit Alfa in a huff to the dismay and embarrassment of Ligier!

Ford, another powerful and loyal supporter of Motor Sport, supplied two types of engine. Their much-improved 1½ litre turbomotor went exclusively to the Benetton team, who'd used BMW power in 1986, and their expanded 'Son of DFV' 3½ litre to the Tyrrell and other 'normally aspirated' teams.

So, with the mechanical scene set, enter the top drivers — differently arranged! Stefan Johansson to McLaren from Ferrari. Martin Brundle to Zakspeed from Tyrrell. Nakajima, the first ever Japanese Grand Prix driver, to Lotus (who had also had a major sponsor change from long-standing JPS to Camel), Derek Warwick from Brabham and Eddie Cheever from oblivion — both to Arrows. Thierry Boutsen from Arrows to Benetton. And, of the likely winners by no means the least, Gerhard Berger to Ferrari from Benetton — for whom he'd won his and their first Grand Prix in Mexico 1986.

As we surveyed the prospects for 1987 they had never looked brighter. At the very least nine drivers looked capable of winning Grands Prix; Prost, Johansson, Mansell, Piquet, Senna, Fabi, Boutsen, Alboreto and Berger. Maybe Warwick and Cheever too. But which of them would be consistent enough to become World Champion?

Williams, McLaren, Benetton, and Ferrari with greatly improved cars and two top drivers all seemed to be in with a chance for the prestigious Constructors' Championship.

But expectations are one thing — actuality is another. The first Grand Prix of the year, the Brazilian in the heat of Rio on 12th April, was to be the beginning of a season to remember!

But whilst their engines might be different all the cars would be racing on the same type of tyre — Goodyear. At the end of 1986 Pirelli had announced their withdrawal from Grand Prix racing — a withdrawal quickly followed by a similar statement from Goodyear due to their need to make drastic economies to fight off a take-over bid. For a while the teams in a state of near panic, faced the prospect of no tyres but this potential disaster was averted when Goodyear relented. Once more they had saved the sport albeit with the entirely reasonable provisos that they must be the sole supplier and that the teams must pay. Which they thankfully agreed to do.

There were other major changes, notably two dramatic designer moves. The brilliant John Barnard, whose McLaren designs had won five World Championships and twenty-eight Grands Prix since 1980, sensationally

BRAZIL

12th April 1987
Circuit: Jacarepagua, Rio de Janeiro

FIVE months after the last Grand Prix, in Australia 1986, the Formula One teams packed their new cars, assembled their manpower and set off to Brazil, full of hope and expectation, for the first of 1987's sixteen World Championship races. Before them lay seven months of ceaseless globe-trotting, money-spending, effort in fifteen countries to gain the richest and most prestigious rewards in Motor Sport, the Drivers' and Constructors' World Championships, plus, for the first time, special awards for the top Driver and Constructor in the new 3½ litre normally-aspirated (non turbocharged) category.

The trip to Rio de Janeiro is one of the longest of the year. Some twelve hours in the plane and when you get there it is a scene of extreme contrasts. At one end of the spectrum the blazing 120 degree heat from an incandescent sun, the glorious Copacabana and Ipanema beaches, the even more glorious Brazilian girls and the incredible restaurants where platoons of waiters, carrying drawn swords laden with cooked meats, carve towering piles of protein on to your plate. Corcovado Mountain with its overwhelming, 38 metre high, statue of Christ the Redeemer blessing and dominating the whole of Rio. The distinctively vast Sugar Loaf Rock and the awesome Maracana Stadium.

But that's the good news. The bad news is the literally frightening amount of violence and mugging — wear a plastic watch, don't carry a wallet and keep your credit card in your sock! — the depressing mass poverty and, as a minor irritation, the dilapidated, alcohol-fuelled hire cars.

The 3.13 mile Jacarepagua circuit is hardly beautiful — flat as a pancake it writhes its way through swampy land which hosts a virulent mosquito whose bite can and does put people into hospital for fever-ridden days on end.

But never mind. The longed-for Grand Prix season of 1987 was beginning there, even if it was in an atmosphere of acrimony. FISA, the governing body of Motor Sport, had decided to levy a sliding scale of fees for Drivers' Super Licences — without which they cannot race — according to points gained in 1986. That meant varying levels from $825 for new or point-less drivers to some $12,000 for Prost, Mansell and Piquet. The result was serious talk of a drivers' strike resolved only after much muscle flexing and an uneasy FISA-loaded compromise. Not a happy start.

Mansell — pole position and posting his season's intentions.

But at ten o'clock on Friday, 10th April all that was at least temporarily forgotten as the first car rolled out of the pit lane for practice. Practice as opposed to qualifying involves one and a half hours of high-speed activity from ten o'clock to eleven-thirty on the Friday and Saturday mornings followed by one hour of timed (to one-thousandth of a second) qualifying runs from one o'clock until two for the starting grid positions. In the morning sessions it's a case of checking fuel consumption, setting up the cars' suspensions and brakes, adjusting a myriad of other mechanical things, and, for the drivers, sorting out racing lines and braking points. In the afternoon it's go for the best time; the higher up the grid you are the clearer a circuit you'll have when the race begins!

The Williams team began where they left off. When Friday's timed session finished it was Nigel Mansell in pole position, for the fifth time in his career, with a superb lap, in 1 min. 26.13 sec. — a mere six-tenths of a second slower than Senna's 1986 pole time in spite of having limited boost pressure and race tyres as opposed to 1986's super-sticky qualifying specials. With Piquet second and Senna third the top three were thus Honda powered — to the accompaniment of dark mutterings in the pit lane about the Japanese having 'obviously' found a way to overcome the four-bar turbo boost limit! And, talking of technicalities, Lotus had decided, after some four years of experimentation and development, to concentrate on their unique 'Active' suspension which replaces the conventional springs and shock absorbers with computer-controlled hydraulic rams. A courageous step; if it worked they'd be unbeatable. If it didn't they'd be in real trouble. In Brazil it wasn't yet perfect.

With speeds of well over 200 miles an hour on the long straight paralleling Jacarepagua's sole, but enormous, grandstand which holds some 100,000 cheering, chanting, flag waving and generally over-the-top Brazilians, and with the notoriously abrasive surface and searing temperatures to contend with, it was obvious that tyres were going to be a key factor in the Brazilian Grand Prix. Smooth driving and mechanical sympathy could (and would) decide the day. Even so at least two stops for tyres were expected.

Tyres then were a worry. So, too, were the new-for-'87 'pop-off' valves which prevent the turbo boost pressures from rising too high. Most of the teams were complaining violently about their unpredictability — 'popping off' too early and losing as much as 200 horsepower. But McLaren weren't. Typically the Woking-based team had diligently worked away all winter to perfect their TAG engines' set up at maximum of 3.6 bar, well below the upper limit. Typically too their cautiously thorough preparation would earn them rich rewards . . .

So, on Sunday morning when the traditional final half-hour of practice began the so-called 'warm-up' even though it happens three

| Jacarepagua circuit — on race day a colourful swamp. | 'They're off' — well nearly! |

Teo Fabi — turbo failure ended his race early.

Team Analysis

McLAREN

Overwhelmingly successful first time out for the new Steve Nicholls-designed MP4/3 car with much revised TAG V6 engine. Complete vindication (not that it was needed!) for the usual McLaren policy of concentrating on the best race set-up in practice rather than striving for best starting grid positions. A dominant win for Alain Prost. Third place for Stefan Johansson in his first McLaren drive. Leadership in both the Drivers' and Constructors' Championships. Not bad for starters!

TYRRELL

Back to normally-aspirated engines (3½ litre V8 Ford DFZ) in an effort to win the 'Non turbo' Driver and Constructor 1987 season awards. After qualifying ten seconds off the pace — but easily the best of the 3½ litre cars — an excellent tenth place for Jonathan Palmer. Phillipe Streiff eleventh despite nausea attacks. Palmer and the new DG 016 cars led the 'B class' Championships.

WILLIAMS

A disappointing race. After dominating practice — Mansell pole and Piquet second — and having Piquet lead, both cars afflicted by over-heating — partly due to rubbish-blocked radiators — and heavy tyre wear. Second place and fastest lap for Piquet. A lucky sixth for Mansell, a lap down, after a total rear tyre deflation. So near yet so far . . .

BRABHAM

All new, good looking, BT56 car with development of unsuccessful 1986 BMW 'lie down' engine. Last minute recruitment of Italian Andrea de Cesaris ('de Crasheris!') to the dismay of No. 1 driver, fellow countryman Riccardo Patrese. Patrese an encouraging seventh for much of the race before retiring with perforated radiator. De Cesaris out with transmission defect. Not good but better than 1986.

McLaren's new designer and McLaren's new driver — Steve Nichols and Stefan Johansson.

ZAKSPEED

1987 cars not yet ready for new recruit Martin Brundle and 'back to Zakspeed from Arrows' Christian Danner. Steady run to ninth for Danner. Misery for Brundle — multiple problems in practice, retirement on lap fifteen (turbo) and out-qualified by Jonathan Palmer in his previous team — Tyrrell! Maximum effort needed to ready 1987 cars for San Marino GP.

LOTUS

New 99T car with Honda engine and pioneering 'Active' suspension for Ayrton Senna and new Japanese driver Satoru Nakajima. Typically super drive from third on the grid by Senna, mostly running strong second until motor tightened to cause retirement mere eleven laps from end. Mature race by Nakajima to finish seventh — just out of points — in first GP. Team clearly heading for victory if revolutionary suspension perfected.

Martin Brundle getting used to Zakspeed turbo power.

AGS

One ugly 3½ litre Ford DFZ-powered car for GP debut of Frenchman Pascal Fabre. Predictably uncompetitive due to newness of both car and driver but twelfth place, six laps adrift, in spite of gearbox problems.

MARCH

Welcome 'Works' return to Formula One after long absence. Definitive 'Grand Prix' design not ready so Formula 3000-specification car with 3½ litre Ford DFZ motor for talented Italian Ivan Capelli to satisfy Formula One Constructors Association (FOCA) rules despite known inability to complete race distance (insufficient fuel tankage). Car withdrawn after practice following multiple engine breakages.

ARROWS

Season started with strongest-ever team. Very impressive all-new Ross Brawn-designed A10 car with Megatron (BMW) turbo engine. Hungry veteran GP drivers Derek Warwick and Eddie Cheever. Warwick qualified excellent eighth and ran strong sixth before blowing motor on lap twenty. Cheever also very encouraging sixth before retiring (engine) with only nine laps to go. In Brazil Arrows looked good for '87.

Ayrton Senna — at home in Brazil but not yet happy with 'Active' suspension.

BENETTON

First race with much improved Ford V6 turbo motor (used by defunct Haas-Lola team in 1986) and Goodyear tyres. All new car designed by brilliant Rory Byrne and driven by introverted Teo Fabi and ex-Arrows, vastly under-rated, Belgian Thierry Boutsen. Fabi qualified excellent fifth and ran third before early turbo failure. Boutsen fulfilled promise by briefly leading and finishing fifth despite puncture. Benetton returned to Witney HQ with heads held high.

OSELLA

Another miracle of mind over money with the appearance of one under-financed, under powered (Alfa V8 turbo) car from enthusiast Enzo Osella driven by sensible ex-Formula Three Italian Alex Caffi. Yet again Osella failed to finish — engine problems on lap twenty. But determination to soldier on had to be admired.

Derek Warwick in the new Ross Brawn Arrows A10.

MINARDI

New M186 car with revised Motori-Moderni V6 turbo motor qualified reasonable fifteenth and sixteenth in hands of under-rated Alessandro Nannini and unimpressive Spanish newcomer Adrian Campos. Nannini spun out of contention with rear suspension failure on lap seventeen. Campos (after forgetting to insert ear plugs!) black-flagged and excluded for breaking start rules.

FERRARI

Depressing debut for all-new F187 with 90 degree V6 engine under control of new Technical Director, Englishman John Barnard. Inefficient aerodynamics caused lack of grip and poor handling. New driver Gerhard Berger qualified and finished (fourth) ahead of established Michele Alboreto (eighth). Obvious need for midnight oil at Maranello if team to shine before fanatical aficionados on home ground at next GP — San Marino.

LIGIER

Although entered the French team, with their drivers Rene Arnoux and Piercarlo Ghinzani, failed to appear as a result of Arnoux publicly criticising the team's Alfa-Romeo turbo motors. Alfa, who allegedly wanted out anyway, angrily withdrew leaving irascible Guy Ligier to cast around for replacement power and start a lawsuit for damages.

'They're off' — start of the '87 season in Brazil.

hours before the race! — the expectation was for a Williams walk-over. Fastest in qualifying by a daunting two seconds, with Mansell and Piquet as drivers, with vast experience of Honda power and with refined but largely unchanged developments of their 1986 all-conquering cars who, from the other much changed teams, could stop them?

McLaren could! For in the warm-up it was the all-too-familiar-from-the-past story of 'Professor' Alain Prost fastest in race set-up. Which, brilliant as he is, few would have predicted, as his car was absolutely new, little tested and a very long way from being fully developed.

As I looked at my monitor and listened to the sun-baked multitudes of Senna and Piquet factions trying to out-shout their rivals I gloomily wondered whether the Brazilian TV producer would let the World see anyone else! I needn't have worried . . .

When the lights turned to green Brazil temporarily went mad as Nelson Piquet, winner in 1983 and '86, shot to the front ahead of Senna with the Benettons of Fabi and Boutsen out-dragging Mansell's Williams and Prost's McLaren. But on only the seventh lap Nelson powered into the pits and out of the lead with the twin problems that were to decide the race — rubbish and tyres. Spectator-generated rubbish in the radiator side pods which sent the engine temperatures soaring, and the need for new tyres induced by the heat and the abrasive track.

From then on the story of the Brazilian Grand Prix was one of constant tyre and place changes as driver after driver rocketed into the pit lane for a new set of Goodyear 'boots' and/or for assorted litter to be frenziedly pulled away from the cars' radiators. As they did so the race order changed lap by lap. First Piquet led. Then Senna. Then, very significantly, Prost, up from fifth on the grid. Then Piquet again. Close behind them the two Benettons were going superbly with both Fabi and Boutsen in the top five until Fabi retired with turbo problems. Mansell fought up to second before his pit stop. Then Boutsen took his place revelling in the magnificent handling of his Benetton. Berger, fourth in his Ferrari, was (despite handling problems) out-driving his team mate Michele Alboreto. Senna was unhappy too, finding the Lotus' 'Active' suspension a bit too active for his liking! But nevertheless the brilliant Brazilian held second place for much of the race until his engine gave up with only eleven laps to go.

On lap twenty-one out of sixty-one the

Nigel Mansell — 'off' in '86, sixth in '87.

masterly Alain Prost re-took the lead after his first tyre stop — and he never lost it even when he stopped again for his second set of tyres on lap thirty-seven. His win was the twenty-sixth of his career and made him the second most successful Grand Prix driver in

Prost in superb form — a Brazilian 'hat-trick'.

Jacarepagua rubbish didn't stop Nelson — second in his homeland.

the history of the World Championship — second only to Jackie Stewart with twenty-seven wins. Alain won for the reason that he always wins. He drove as fast as he had to, and no faster. He drove sympathetically to preserve his tyres, making two stops where others made three. And he did it in a new, under-developed car he'd never raced before! His fourth Brazilian win in six years was one of his best ever.

Only three other drivers went the full distance; Piquet, Johansson and Berger, for both the other point scorers, Boutsen a fine fifth in his first race for Benetton and Mansell, sixth in spite of a time consuming puncture, were lapped. Johansson and Berger each drove outstanding races for their new teams and could be expected to go even better in future races.

With both their men in the top three places and with a very comforting six point lead in the Constructors' Championship McLaren quietly announced their intention to spend the next three weeks before the San Marino GP testing and developing their new car 'to make it really work' — a depressing prospect for the other teams and they returned to ponder where they'd gone wrong and what to do about it.

BRAZIL GRAND PRIX

Winner: Alain Prost, McLaren MP4/3-3   *Fastest Lap:* Nelson Piquet, 119.926 mph

GRID POSITION		RESULTS			WORLD CHAMPIONSHIP				
No.	Driver	Pos.	Driver	Car	Drivers	Pts	Constructors		Pts
5	Mansell	1	Prost	McLaren-TAG MP4/3-3	1. Prost	9	1. McLaren-TAG		13
6	Piquet	2	Piquet	Williams-Honda FW11B/2	2. Piquet	6	2. Williams-Honda		7
12	Senna	3	Johansson	McLaren-TAG MP4/3-2	3. Johansson	4	3. Ferrari		4
19	Fabi	4	Berger	Ferrari F187-095	4. Berger	3	4. Benetton-Ford		2
1	Prost	5	Boutsen	Benetton-Ford B187-03	5. Boutsen	2			
20	Boutsen	6	Mansell	Williams-Honda FW11B/3	6. Mansell	1			
28	Berger	7	Nakajima	Lotus-Honda 99T/1					
17	Warwick	8	Alboreto	Ferrari F187-096	JIM CLARK CUP		COLIN CHAPMAN CUP		
27	Alboreto	9	Danner	Zakspeed 861/3	1. Palmer	9	1. Tyrrell-Cosworth		15
2	Johansson	10	Palmer	Tyrrell-Cosworth DG/016-2	2. Streiff	6	2. AGS-Cosworth		4
7	Patrese	11	Streiff	Tyrrell-Cosworth DG/016-1	3. Fabre	4			
11	Nakajima	12	Fabre	AGS-Cosworth JH22/02					
8	De Cesaris								
18	Cheever								
24	Nannini								
23	Campos								
10	Danner								
3	Palmer								
9	Brundle								
4	Streiff								
21	Caffi								
14	Fabre								
16	Capelli								

SAN MARINO

3rd May 1987
Circuit: Imola near Bologna

'HE'S alright' said Sid. 'He knows who he is, where he is and who I am.' Which is apparently a good sign when you've just had a colossal, high speed crash. 'Sid' was professor E. S. Watkins, President of the FISA Medical Committee, and 'he' was Nelson Piquet who'd spun off the 200 miles an hour approach to the acute Tosa corner at Imola in his Williams-Honda and slammed into the guard-rail half way through Friday's timed practice for the San Marino Grand Prix.

It may be called the San Marino Grand Prix but it is really a second Italian Grand Prix for the tiny self-governing Principality is fifty miles away from the Imola circuit which it uses 'as a matter of convenience' since San Marino itself does not have a suitable road system for a Grand Prix!

The Goodyear service — at its very best at Imola.

Nelson Piquet 'alright' before his terrifying practice crash.

The Imola circuit, scene of Europe's first Grand Prix of 1987, is on the flat Lombardy Plain some twenty miles east of Bologna and less than fifty miles from Modena, the home of Ferrari. Indeed its correct title is the Autodromo Dino Ferrari for it is named in memory of the late son of the great Enzo Ferrari. It forms a truly superb setting for a World Championship Grand Prix, a setting to which the Ferrari-worshipping 'Tifosi' flock in their tens of thousands to shout, scream and flag-wave in support of the team which matters more to them than all the others put together.

Imola's anti-clockwise 3.13 mile lap, shaped roughly like an ankle boot, has two super-fast stretches which are good for some 200 miles an hour. It includes uphill and downhill sections (unusual at today's GP circuits), three chicanes to slow things down and a variety of sweeping left and right bends. The drivers like Imola and the spectators love it. In fact but for one thing, it is immensely popular with everyone because its facilities are the best there are. Magnificent garages with their own washrooms and toilets. Modern, permanent grandstands. A wide and safe pit lane (although, being Italy, far too many unauthorised people wangle passes to get into it!), excellent telephone and telex rooms, a very good restaurant and Press room and, for the TV commentators, an impressive studio for post-race driver interviews on the roof of the pits complex right next to the commentary boxes. Luxury indeed! The one thing that nobody likes, incidentally, is the journey to the airport after the race when everyone in Italy seems to be trying to use the congested country roads to get to the Autostrada. It took the BBC team 4½ hours to do three miles this year — but we all have problems. Add pasta, wine, sunshine and the best dressed girls in motor racing and Imola takes a lot of beating!

Practice at Imola is always crucial because the San Marino GP is the greatest challenge of all in terms of fuel consumption. The race is 188 miles long and, at an average speed of some 120 mph, making the mandatory maximum of 195 litres of fuel last the distance demand fast, smooth driving and cautious tactics. Which is undoubtedly why Alain Prost had won at Imola for the last three years (although excluded in 1985 when his McLaren was found to be two kilograms under weight after he'd run out of fuel on his victory lap).

Berger's supreme test — his first Ferrari race in Italy.

But in the afternoon qualifying sessions it's a case of flat out for pole and that is when Piquet inexplicably lost it on Friday. With the fastest time half way through the session he almost literally flew off the circuit and the fact that he was able to get out of the car when it finally stopped was the clearest possible

Nigel Mansell's first win of '87 was the eighth of his career.

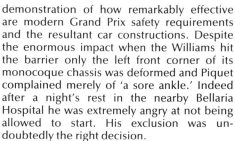

Mansell views practice times — Senna gets pole.

'Best dressed girls in motor racing' — I wonder what the marshal is thinking?

demonstration of how remarkably effective are modern Grand Prix safety requirements and the resultant car constructions. Despite the enormous impact when the Williams hit the barrier only the left front corner of its monocoque chassis was deformed and Piquet complained merely of 'a sore ankle.' Indeed after a night's rest in the nearby Bellaria Hospital he was extremely angry at not being allowed to start. His exclusion was undoubtedly the right decision.

More drama greeted us on Saturday morning. Alarmed by excessive blistering on the shoulders of their tyres and the possibility that Piquet's accident might have been caused by a deflation Goodyear withdrew all the 'covers' they had issued to the teams. At the same time they chartered a plane and flew in over 400 replacement tyres from their Wolverhampton factory. They arrived in Bologna at 0400 on Saturday morning only for the Goodyear people to discover that it was a public holiday and that the Customs were conspicuous by their absence! Vigorous activity, forcefully assisted by Enzo Ferrari's English secretary,

the formidable Brenda Vernor, saved the day — and the race. Very wise and responsible action by Goodyear as a result of which there were no further tyre problems.

Qualifying continued on the new rubber for the 26 cars which included six 'first timers'. The new and very effective Ralph Bellamy designed 3½ litre Lola for Frenchman Philippe Alliot (ex RAM and Ligier). The 'proper' 3½ litre Grand Prix March for Ivan Capelli. The new 1987 Zakspeed for Martin Brundle. A second old Osella for Italian new boy Gabriele Tarquini. And, to everyone's amazement, two Megatron-powered Ligiers for Rene Arnoux

Team Analysis

McLAREN

Alain Prost, who went to Imola having won for the last three years (although excluded in 1985), qualified a strong third and was confident of a fourth victory. But it was not to be as alternator failure took him out of second place on lap 15. Stefan Johansson drove to a determined fourth from eighth on the grid in spite of an unscheduled stop to replace his nose cone. Prost and Johansson second and third in the Drivers' Championship. McLaren now tied for the lead (with Williams) in the Constructors' contest.

TYRRELL

Philippe Streiff qualified twenty-first and 'best in class' (3.5 litre). Jonathan Palmer, now contracted to the team for the entire season, twenty-fourth on grid due to an elusive misfire. On race day, Ken Tyrrell's sixty-third birthday, Palmer led the non-turbo class in fourteenth place until retiring on lap 49 (clutch). Streiff finished excellent eighth to win his class. Tyrrell team increase lead in both non-turbo Championships.

WILLIAMS

A Grand Prix of mixed fortunes for the Didcot team. Mammoth crash for Piquet during Friday qualifying session when holding pole position. Subsequently deemed unfit to race by medical authorities. Second on the grid for Mansell followed by magnificent race which he dominated. Led all but six of the fifty-nine laps, won his eighth Grand Prix by a commanding twenty-seven seconds and took the lead in Drivers' Championship. Piquet drops to fourth place but Williams now tie for lead in Constructors' Championship with McLaren.

BRABHAM

Heartening signs of a return to form with the team's best race for a very long time. Usual unimpressive performance by De Cesaris (fourteenth on grid. Spun twice and out of race lap forty). But Patrese excellent. Qualified seventh and tigered up to totally unexpected second challenging Mansell until broken alternator forced retirement four laps from end. New 'Committee Design' car (John Baldwin, Sergio Rhinland and David North) showed great promise.

ZAKSPEED

New 1987 'Interim' car for Martin Brundle (still with same wings and suspension as '86). Despondent Brundle qualified fifteenth after multiple practice problems but with steady drive finished encouraging fifth to score team's first Championship points. Danner started eighteenth and finished excellent seventh in 1986 car. Underfunded Zakspeed team's best race yet.

LOTUS

Further improvement following intensive development of innovatory 'Active' suspension. Excellent result with both drivers scoring World Championship points. Senna takes first-ever 'Active' pole in Lotus-Honda 99T (and his career

sixteenth) followed by encouraging race to finish second after briefly leading twice. Nakajima qualified twelfth but started last from the pit lane following withdrawal from grid with flat battery. Finished fine sixth in only second Grand Prix to score first-ever championship point by Japanese driver. Senna now fourth equal (with Piquet) in Drivers' Championship. Lotus tie for third with Ferrari in Constructors' table.

Alas poor Warwick ran out of fuel.

AGS

Pascal Fabre, now one of five drivers in the 3.5 litre class, continued his record of race finishes with thirteenth place six laps behind the winner (as in Brazil) despite spinning and nearly forcing Alliot (Lola) out of contention.

MARCH

Debut of the brand new 3.5 litre Ford DFZ-powered GP car for the personable Ivan Capelli (in the presence of millionaire Japanese sponsor Akari Akagi of Leyton House). Formula 3000 car with 3.3 litre DFL sports car engine also used for practice. Meeting regarded as extended test session by the Ian Phillips-managed team. Capelli qualified twenty-third and retired in eighteenth place on lap nineteen due, of all things, to a broken rotor arm!

ARROWS

Team financial position for 1987 further strengthened following agreement to share previously exclusive Megatron engine with Ligier on joint-development basis. Derek Warwick qualified tenth and drove excellent race up to fifth when fuel ran out on lap 56 despite gauge showing sufficient for two and a half more laps. Eddie Cheever ninth on the grid and retired when ninth on lap 49 (head gasket).

BENETTON

Another 'almost there' race. Fourth on the grid for Teo Fabi and eleventh for Thierry Boutsen despite many problems saw the team looking good for the race. After early setbacks Fabi fought up to excellent fourth only to retire (lap 52) with engine failure. His consolation, though, was fastest lap of the race. Boutsen underlined his considerable Brazilian promise by steadily improving to fifth place only to retire on lap 49 (engine). With reliability Benetton would be there.

Lotus bodies catch the sun in San Marino.

OSELLA

First GP drive for ex-Formula 3000 Gabriele Tarquini who qualified twenty-sixth and ran last in weary car until retiring on lap 27 (gearbox). The impressive Alex Caffi, in only his third GP qualified well at twentieth and, unusually for an Osella driver, finished in twelfth place, albeit five laps down.

MINARDI

As so often in the past the Minardi cars, although much improved over 1986, suffered from unreliability. The impressive Alessandro Nannini only managed one practice session in which he qualified sixteenth with team mate Adrian Campos a surprising seventeenth. In the race both drivers retired. Nannini on lap 26 (engine) and Campos on lap 31 (gearbox).

LIGIER

After 'Force Majeur' non-start at Brazil an unexpected appearance at Imola with two Megatron-powered cars (see 'Arrows') following three weeks non-stop work to re-engineer the previously Alfa-Romeo engined monocoques. Team clearly delighted with their new motors but understandably not fully prepared. Thirteenth and nineteenth places on the grid for Arnoux and Ghinzani. Arnoux failed to start following irremedial suspension problem on race day. Ghinzani retired lap eight (dodgy handling) but Ligier were back and in good heart.

FERRARI

Improvement at Imola following furious activity at Maranello and Shalford (John Barnard's Surrey R&D base) to make the F187s race winners. Berger and Alboreto shared third row of the starting grid (despite Alboreto hay fever problems) and both ran strongly, fourth and fifth, in opening stages of race. Impressive Berger retired lap 17 (low boost pressure).

Philippe Alliot an excellent tenth in the new Lola-Cosworth.

Alboreto had race long scrap with Senna to finish third after leading race for three laps. Ferrari tie for third (with Lotus) in Constructors' Championship. Development pressure to continue!

LOLA

First Grand Prix appearance of very effective Ralph Bellamy designed and 3.5 litre Ford DFZ powered car for Frenchman Philippe Alliot (ex RAM and Ligier) under control of experienced Gerard Larrousse (ex Renault and Ligier). Excellent performance to start twenty-second (second fastest 3.5 litre) and finish tenth (second in class to Streiff) in spite of being delayed by Fabre spin. A very impressive, enthusiastic and well organised team offering a real future challenge to the Tyrrells in the non-turbo class.

Alliot passes Fabre the hard way.

and Piercarlo Ghinzani, the French team having done a fantastic job to re-engineer their cars in only three weeks to take the new motors in place of their original Alfa-Romeo engines.

Practice at Imola made history. The first-ever pole position for a car with 'Active' suspension — Ayrton Senna's Lotus-Honda 99T. It was Senna's third successive pole position at Imola (only eight-tenths of a second slower than his 1986 time with qualifying boost and tyres) and the sixteenth of his short career in Formula One. Although Lotus said the new system still wasn't 100% right there clearly wasn't much wrong with it! Second on the grid was Nigel Mansell. Third (although a whisker slower than the non-starting Piquet) was a very happy and confident Alain Prost and a magnificent fourth was Teo Fabi in his Benetton-Ford. To the delight of the 'Tifosi', Berger and Alboreto made it an all-Ferrari third row whilst to the surprise of everyone Patrese's Brabham-BMW was seventh — a portent of things to come!

The start of the San Marino Grand Prix was aborted before it even happened. With the grid formed and ready to go at the end of the parade lap the arms of Cheever, Boutsen and Brundle waved agitatedly out of their cockpits — they'd stalled their engines. So Grand Prix's new starter, Belgian Roland Bruynseraede, wisely sent them round again. All except Satoru Nakajima who's Lotus-Honda was

taken to the pit lane with a flat battery, Arnoux who'd withdrawn with suspension problems and, of course, Piquet.

Senna led on lap one but on lap two Nigel Mansell calmly drove round the Lotus to take the lead and dominate the race even more than Prost had dominated Brazil. Of the 59 laps (one less than originally intended due to the extra parade lap) Mansell led 53. There was a time, in his Lotus days, when Nigel was regarded as impetuous and unable to handle pressure. But not this time. This was a cool, calm drive by the best man in the best car controlling the race from the front to win by a very impressive 27 seconds. His eighth Grand Prix victory put him into the lead of the Drivers' Championship and Williams into a shared lead of the Constructors' Championship with McLaren.

Behind him Prost rapidly and confidently moved up to second playing his usual waiting game ahead of a glorious nose-to-tail battle for third between Senna's Lotus and the two Ferraris of Alboreto and Berger. Until lap fifteen when, to the open delight of the partisan crowd, Prost's race ended with a failed alternator. His San Marino luck had to run out sometime and this was it.

Next to disappear was Gerhard Berger with failing turbo boost (lap 17). With Alboreto now second Riccardo Patrese moved up to

fourth behind Senna who led Johansson and a rejuvenated Derek Warwick in the impressive new Arrows-Megatron. On lap 22 Mansell shot into his pit for an early tyre change caused by the fact that a wheel balance weight had come off — at which point, for three glorious laps as far as the crowd was concerned, Alboreto's Ferrari led a Grand Prix in Italy! Then, for two laps, Senna took over at the front whilst Alboreto pitted but, on lap 27 Mansell was back in the lead position he was to retain to the end.

But now second place was held by an inspired Riccardo Patrese in the new Brabham. He'd sliced past Alboreto and Senna and was actually catching Mansell until he dived into his pit, later than most, for new Goodyears on lap 37. Rejoining in fourth place he did it again motoring confidently and firmly past the warring Alboreto and Senna back to second place on lap 44. Only fifteen laps to go and it seemed that Brabham were back after a season of misery and failure in 1986.

Meantime with Senna third followed by Alboreto, Johansson and Warwick, Teo Fabi was charging in the Benetton-Ford. After a slow start and a stop for a new front wing end plate he picked off car after car to take a

Johansson on his way to fourth place.

determined fourth place behind Mansell, Senna and Alboreto on lap 51, only to retire the next lap with a failed engine. His consolation though was that during his charge he made the fastest lap of the race at 126.34 mph. (Fabi's team mate Boutsen had gone out with the same complaint after an excellent drive from eleventh to fifth.)

At almost the same time what, for me, was the drive of the day — Patrese's — petered out as his alternator gave up. That elevated the race long Alboreto-versus-Senna confrontation to second and third — resolved in favour of Senna when the Italian's boost (like team mate Berger's) withered away.

Stefan Johansson was the only other driver to go the full distance with Brundle and Nakajima making history in fifth and sixth places; the first World Championship points for the hard-trying Zakspeed team and the first ever for a Japanese driver. No doubt they celebrated!

In the 3.5 litre class Streiff won with a fine eighth place overall followed by Alliot (10th) and Fabre (13th). The Frenchman's win put the Tyrrell team well ahead in both the 3.5 litre class Championships.

Finally a sad hard-luck story. With two laps

Streiff's Tyrrell picked up first place in the non-turbo category.

to go and a fuel gauge showing 2½ laps left Derek Warwick ran out of petrol in a points scoring fifth place.

So, with two rounds gone and fourteen to go, the honours were even between the Williams and McLaren teams. But Lotus, Ferrari, Benetton and Arrows were all gathering strength.

Nigel Mansell now led the Drivers' World Championship, facing the next round in Belgium, where he'd won in 1986!

SAN MARINO GRAND PRIX

Winner: Nigel Mansell, Williams FW11B/3   *Fastest Lap:* Teo Fabi, 126.338 mph

GRID POSITION		RESULTS			WORLD CHAMPIONSHIP				
No.	Driver	Pos.	Driver	Car	Drivers	Pts	Constructors		Pts
12	Senna	1	Mansell	Williams-Honda FW11B/3	1. Mansell	10	1. McLaren-TAG		16
5	Mansell	2	Senna	Lotus-Honda 99T/4	2. Prost	9	Williams-Honda		16
1	Prost	3	Alboreto	Ferrari F187-096	3. Johansson	7	3. Ferrari		7
19	Fabi	4	Johansson	McLaren-TAG MP4/3-2	4. Piquet	6	Lotus-Honda		7
28	Berger	5	Brundle	Zakspeed 871/1	Senna	6	5. Benetton-Ford		2
27	Alboreto	6	Nakajima	Lotus-Honda 99T/1	6. Alboreto	4	Zakspeed		2
7	Patrese	7	Danner	Zakspeed 861/3	7. Berger	3			
2	Johansson	8	Streiff	Tyrrell-Cosworth DG/016-1	8. Boutsen	2			
18	Cheever	9	Patrese	Brabham-BMW BT56/3	Brundle	2			
17	Warwick	10	Alliot	Lola-Ford LC87/01	10. Nakajima	1			
20	Boutsen	11	Warwick	Arrows Megatron A10/1					
11	Nakajima	12	Caffi	Osella-Alfa FAIH/01/87	**JIM CLARK CUP**		**COLIN CHAPMAN CUP**		
8	De Cesaris	13	Fabre	AGS Cosworth JH22/02	1. Streiff	15	1. Tyrrell-Cosworth		24
9	Brundle				2. Palmer	9	2. AGS-Cosworth		8
24	Nannini				3. Fabre	8	3. Lola-Cosworth		6
23	Campos				4. Alliot	6			
10	Danner								
26	Ghinzani								
21	Caffi								
4	Streiff								
30	Alliot								
16	Capelli								
3	Palmer								
14	Fabre								
22	Tarquini								

BELGIUM

17th May 1987
Circuit: Spa-Francorchamps

THE Grand Prix teams always go to Belgium with mixed feelings. Pleasure with the knowledge that they will again be visiting the glorious green and hilly Ardennes countryside with its beautiful forests, farmland and restaurants! But dismay with the fact that the area's unpredictable weather means that they never know, literally from minute to minute, whether it is going to be wet or dry. Clear blue skies and blazing sunshine seem instantaneously to turn black and disgorge heavy showers of rain, or even hail, which make a lottery out of setting up the cars properly for practice and the race. This year was certainly no exception.

Compensating handsomely for the weather problems, however, is the magnificent Spa-Francorchamps course — the only one of its type in the Grand Prix calendar. Some 4.3 miles long it is entirely composed of public roads specially closed for the race and embraces just about every imaginable type of corner plus the attribute that almost every other modern course lacks — gradient. Today's Spa circuit, first used in 1983, is a shortened version of the historic venue where, from 1924, some of the World's most evocative drivers and cars competed. Pre-war the Mercedes-Benz of Caracciola, Lang and Seaman (who was tragically killed there in 1939) and the Auto-Unions of Stuck and Hasse. Post-war, with the advent of the World Championship series in 1950, the Belgian Grand Prix winners read like a Who's Who of the World's Greatest — amongst them Fangio, Ascari, Brabham, Clark, Stewart, Lauda and Prost.

From the start it is a short dash to the first gear acute right hand hairpin at La Source before the breathtakingly spectacular, 190 miles an hour, plunge downhill to the right/left sweep at Eau Rouge, one of the most exciting sights in Grand Prix racing. To watch the skid plates striking sparks and the drivers taking a millimetre-perfect line into the dip and over the crest without even lifting makes

The 'Professor' thinking it out.

you realise that they really deserve their stratospheric wages! Then uphill via a long over-200 miles an hour climb to the highest point, Les Combes, before dropping down into and across a wooded valley through a series of sweeping left and right hand bends which lead to the gentle climb back through thick woods, the 'Bus Stop' chicane, the pits and La Source. All of it truly a sight to set the pulses racing.

Practice, maddeningly frustrating for the teams because of the changeable weather, was dominated by a supremely confident Nigel Mansell at the top of his form and leading the Drivers' Championship. Skilfully picking the best time to go out when there was a temporary dry line round all or most of the circuit and when he could therefore use slick tyres he was fastest on Friday morning, second fastest to Berger in Friday's qualifying session and fastest on Saturday morning. But it was the final qualifying hour on Saturday afternoon that mattered most and here Nigel was in a class of his own. On a dry track and partly thanks to a special 'qualifying' microchip in his Honda engine's electronic management system, he positively rocketed round to record a searing 1:52.026 minute lap. This was an amazing 2.3 seconds faster than Nelson Piquet's 1986 pole time that had been achieved using the turbo super-boost and the stickiest of qualifying tyres, outlawed in 1987. Everyone was faster on Saturday and when practising finished it was an all-Williams front row for the starting grid with Piquet lining up slightly behind Mansell followed by Senna's

Lotus, Berger, and Alboreto in Ferraris — a heartening sight — and World Champion Alain Prost who, as usual, had concentrated on his race set-up rather than grid position during practice. A decision which, as ever, turned out to be the right one. The Benettons with Boutsen seventh on his home circuit and Fabi ninth, were well up too whilst Patrese, at eighth, was maintaining the vastly improved form the Brabhams had shown at Imola two weeks earlier. Johansson, a low tenth due, he said, to being baulked by Danner on his fast lap, headed the Arrows of Cheever and Warwick whilst the ebullient Ivan Capelli in his March-Ford was the fastest 3½ litre driver at 21st.

On Sunday morning, though, it was the 'Old Firm' at the top during the half hour final practice. Prost first and Johansson second in their McLarens — a fact that was to be more than significant in the race to follow.

When the lights turned to green Mansell made the start of starts to lead Senna and Piquet and by the end of the lap he was well ahead. Behind him though the usual Spa fracas, caused by the closeness of the La Source hairpin to the grid, when Arnoux clouted De Cesaris to end their day's racing. They thought.

But they were wrong. Because at of all places Eau Rouge, on lap two, there was a horrifying crash as Philippe Streiff lost his Tyrrell and slammed it into the barrier at over

Boutsen 'bottoming' his Benetton in Belgium.

Alboretto's Ferrari lifting off — the F187 is a lovely looking racing car.

150 miles an hour. Jonathan Palmer, unsighted by the dust and smoke, unavoidably ran into his team mate. Unbelievably neither of them was hurt although their cars were history. To complete an incident-packed lap Boutsen hit a spinning Berger's Ferrari at the Bus Stop to raise the tally of broken cars to six after less than nine miles of racing. Needless to say the race was stopped.

Some forty minutes later with Arnoux, De Cesaris, Berger, Boutsen and Streiff in their spare cars, but Palmer non-starting, the race began again — for the full forty-three lap distance.

This time Senna took the lead into La Source with a piece of inspired barging between the front row men, Mansell and Piquet. As they lined up for the double right hander at the

Team Analysis

It's Honda which makes the Lotus hump.

McLAREN

A crushing demonstration of all-round superiority. After usual practice concentration on finding best race set-up Prost and Johansson 6th and 10th on grid — but significant fastest and second fastest during race morning half hour final practice. Prost makes fastest lap on way to easy 27th Grand Prix win, despite defunct fuel gauge, equalling fourteen year old Jackie Stewart record and taking World Championship lead. Excellent second place takes Johansson to second in World Championship — having finished in top six in all three 1987 Grands Prix. Two McLaren drivers only ones to go full 43 lap distance — putting their team into commanding Constructors' Championship lead 15 points ahead of no-score Williams.

TYRRELL

Team still affected by misfire problem despite post-Imola testing and attendance of Cosworth engine consultant. Streiff and Palmer 23rd and 24th on grid. Both involved in enormous high speed crash after Eau Rouge which destroys Streiff car although mercifully neither man injured. Streiff courageously takes re-start in spare car to misfire home ninth overall (second in 3½ litre class) and retain Jim Clark Trophy lead. Palmer non-starts (no car). Tyrrell still lead Colin Chapman Trophy contest.

WILLIAMS

A dismal race the team would rather forget after dominant practice. All-Williams start grid front row with Mansell on pole. After leading stopped race Mansell spins off following controversial second race lap one attempt to pass race leader Senna. Piquet leads laps one to nine but retires lap ten (turbo). Mansell rejoins race, retires lap fifteen (accident damage). Mansell down to third in Drivers' Championship and Piquet to fifth.

Nakajima getting better all the time — seventh in Brazil, sixth at Imola, fifth in Belgium.

BRABHAM

Another encouraging race after continued development work by team and BMW engine wizard Paul Rosche. Patrese eighth and De Cesaris thirteenth in practice. Patrese improves to sixth in race following Mansell/Senna fracas but retires lap four (clutch). Eventful day for De Cesaris who re-starts following puncture in first 'race' and drives to fighting third one lap down out of fuel. First 1987 Constructors points for Brabham.

ZAKSPEED

First race in 1987 car for the lofty Danner who complains that it is too small for him! Disappointing 18th (Brundle) and 20th in qualifying. Brundle up to encouraging eighth by lap 18 but out lap 20 (engine). Danner retires lap 10 when 18th (brakes). Still much to do for the capable and enthusiastic, but under-funded, German team who make more of their car than any other team except Ferrari.

LOTUS

More solid achievements by the Hethel team but great disappointment too. From third on grid Senna barges between Mansell/Piquet to take lead at start only to spin off following contentious lap one collision with Mansell. Car undamaged but forced to retire as stuck in sand. Another gritty drive by newcomer Nakajima to fifth place one lap down with impressive third finish in three races (last two in points). Senna now fourth in Drivers' Championship and Lotus third in Constructors' — but massive 22 points behind leaders McLaren.

AGS

Mixed emotions for the little French team. Two nose cones stolen from pit before first practice. Pascal Fabre warned for failing to use mirrors after vigorous protests accompanied by regrets that driver wasn't stolen too! Fabre starts 25th but, unlike most of his rivals, soldiers on to finish 10th overall and third in 3½ litre class — five laps down.

MARCH

Team makes substantial progress at post-Imola Silverstone testing. Capelli miraculously unhurt in multi-roll road car crash, qualifies 21st and top 3½ litre. Takes first start in spare car after real car fails but electrical fault corrected for second start. Retires from excellent eleventh place lap 15 (low oil pressure) when leading class. But with reliability March now in position to win their class.

ARROWS

Considerable inter-race engine development by Megatron technicians. Cheever and Warwick qualify eleventh and twelfth. Warwick improves to ninth by lap seven but immediately retires with burst water hose. Cheever advances steadily to finish excellent fourth, one lap down, and score team's first 1987 points (which qualify them for free travel to all 1988 races). Arrows now looking potential qualifiers for future top-six finishes.

BENETTON

Another 'so near yet so far' race for the immensely popular Witney team, still getting to know their third new car-and-engine combination in three years. Boutsen qualifies seventh

for his home Grand Prix, Fabi ninth. Teo progresses to second and Thierry to fourth before retiring. Boutsen lap 16 (wheel bearing) and Fabi lap 35 (engine). Soon it must all come right . . .

OSELLA

Back to one entry for Alex Caffi who can do no better, with old and outmoded car, than qualify 26th and last and retire on lap twelve (broken fuel pipe) when seventeenth at tail of field. But full marks to the team for their unquenchable enthusiasm in constantly discouraging, under-financed circumstances.

MINARDI

Minardi, like Osella, held back by inadequate funding and a weak engine (Motori Moderni). Nevertheless the very impressive Nannini qualifies excellent fourteenth. Campos nineteenth on grid but fails to start due to low oil pressure. Nannini goes little further — retiring lap two when praiseworthy twelfth (turbo).

LIGIER

Revised front suspension system following San Marino failures on both cars which now need drastic slimming as substantially overweight. Arnoux and Ghinzani qualify 16th and 17th prior to team's best 1987 race so far. Arnoux sixth two laps down scores first Ligier point of year. Ghinzani seventh in one of very few career finishes after five years with Osella. Encouraging progress for the French team after their Alfa-Romeo-to-Megatron engine dramas.

FERRARI

Belgium started well but finished badly. Strong qualifying performances — Berger fourth and Alboreto fifth — followed by race day collapse and gloom. Berger out lap three (engine) after running fifth. Alboreto second laps two to nine but despondently retires lap ten (broken CV joint). New sad Ferrari record — no win since 26 races ago (Germany 1985).

LOLA

Excellent race for the small, efficient and impressive Gerard Larrousse-managed French team. Alliot 20th on grid (second 3.5). Fast reliable race nets eighth place despite Philippe nearly T-boning race leader Prost as rejoins circuit after closing-laps spin. Alliot now second in 3½ litre Drivers' Championship and Lola second in Constructors table.

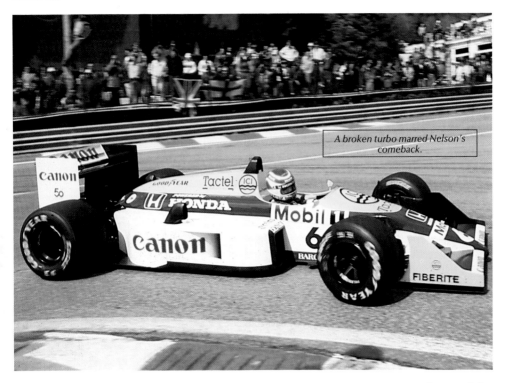

A broken turbo marred Nelson's comeback.

bottom of the circuit, doing some 140 miles an hour, Senna momentarily slowed as he approached a bump where his Lotus 'Active' suspension had gone passive during practice. Immediately Mansell was alongside him and they ran round the long bend together. As they did so, with neither giving way, the two leaders touched and spun in unison into the deep sandy run-off area whilst a gleeful Nelson Piquet sliced past followed by Alboreto and Prost.

Everyone who saw this dramatic coming-together on television had their own views as to who was to blame. The fact is however, no one will ever really know which, if either, of the bitter rivals who had tangled in almost identical circumstances twice before (Australia, '85 and Brazil, '86) , was at fault. Each blamed the other. Mansell subsequently and shamefully assaulted the dignified Senna in his pit garage but irrespective of who was the culprit their clash put the Brazilian out on the spot (bogged down in the sand) and Mansell on lap eighteen with accident damage.

With Berger almost immediately out of the race — lap three: broken piston — Piquet led Alboreto, Prost, Fabi and Boutsen (and a fine sight the multicoloured Benettons made as they raced round together) followed by a rapidly closing Stefan Johansson who had already gained four places.

But on lap ten 'The Professor' was in front. Prost was the leader when Piquet went out with a broken turbo pipe and Alboreto was stranded at Les Combes with a shattered wheel bearing. Fabi was now second with Johansson third and gaining, Boutsen down to fourth (and soon to retire with, like Alboreto, wheel bearing problems), De Cesaris fifth in the Brabham and Cheever sixth.

On lap twenty, less than half way through a race that was now interesting rather than exciting only eleven of the twenty-five starters were left and they were strung out over two laps. Mansell and Piquet were out. Senna, Alboreto and Berger were out. Boutsen, Patrese, Warwick, Nannini and Brundle were out. And so were Campos, Danner, Capelli

Andrea De Cesaris' work place —
he drove a very fine race.

and Caffi. The gruelling Spa-Francorchamps course was certainly living up to its reputation as a car breaker.

But, was the imperturbable Prost, the thinking man's Grand Prix driver in the technician's car, serene and happy in the lead? No he was not. For whilst he reeled off lap after lap at a steady two minutes, plus or minus a few tenths of a second, he was faced by a blank fuel gauge in a race where consumption was almost as critical as it was at Imola. And this was where the superlative McLaren organisation scored again. On his car-to-pit radio Prost coolly requested advice on team-mate Johansson's fuel consumption, as the Swede circulated at an almost identical speed behind him. The answer was satisfactory but just to be safe Alain turned down his boost a bit and concentrated on concentrating — maintaining his rhythm and his 'slow' but more than adequate lap times on his way to making history.

In winning his 27th Grand Prix — which he easily did by some 25 seconds — Prost equalled the fourteen year old record of three times World Champion Jackie Stewart who was there to see the Frenchman do it. 'No regrets,' said Jackie 'I've held the record longer than anyone — in fact I've held it longer than it took me to get it and if I'm going to lose it to anyone I'd rather do so to Prost who is my driver of the decade'. A generous and sincere tribute.

But in many ways the drive of the Belgian Grand Prix was that of Andrea De Cesaris. Many is the time I've criticised him or commented aghast at yet another of his car-destroying incidents but Spa saw the Italian at his very best in his rejuvenated Brabham-BMW. By lap 30 he was third ahead of the soon-to-retire Fabi and, uniquely without a tyre stop, he stayed there to the end in spite of running out of fuel on his last lap and courageously, but unnecessarily, trying to push his car over the line. Brabham were indeed again a force to contend with.

Once again though McLaren were supreme. Only Prost and Johannson went the full

No opposition for Prost on his way to his record-equalling 27th victory.

distance to move, very deservedly, into first and second places in the Drivers' Championship with McLaren now fifteen points ahead of the downcast Williams team, in the constructors table.

Behind the McLarens De Cesaris (third), Cheever (fourth) and Arnoux (sixth) scored the first 1987 points for Brabham, Arrows and Ligier whilst a fine fifth was that of the astounding Satoru Nakajima (Lotus) who had now not only finished in all his first three Grands Prix but had done so in ascending order of places — scoring twice in the process. At this rate he would win the British Grand Prix!

Philippe Alliot, three laps down with an excellent eighth place for Lola, won the 3½ litre class from the brave Philippe Streiff and Fabre in spite of the nearly harpooning race leader Prost as he rejoined the circuit after a spin in the closing stages. Which, come to think of it, is about the only thing that could have stopped Alain!

Back, then, to base they went again. This time to consider the fact that the next Grand Prix was Monaco where Prost had won for the last three years!

BELGIAN GRAND PRIX

Winner: Alain Prost, McLaren MP4/3-3   Fastest Lap: Alain Prost, 132.513 mph

GRID POSITION		RESULTS			WORLD CHAMPIONSHIP				
No.	Driver	Pos.	Driver	Car	Drivers	Pts	Constructors		Pts
5	Mansell	1	Prost	McLaren-TAG MP4/3-3	1. Prost	18	1. McLaren-TAG		31
6	Piquet	2	Johansson	McLaren-TAG MP4/3-2	2. Johansson	13	2. Williams-Honda		16
12	Senna	3	De Cesaris	Brabham-BMW BT56/2	3. Mansell	10	3. Lotus-Honda		9
28	Berger	4	Cheever	Arrows-Megatron A10/2	4. Piquet	6	4. Ferrari		7
27	Alboreto	5	Nakajima	Lotus-Honda 99T/1	Senna	6	5. Brabham-BMW		4
1	Prost	6	Arnoux	Ligier-Megatron JS29B/3	6. Alboreto	4	6. Arrows-Megatron		3
20	Boutsen	7	Ghinzani	Ligier-Megatron JS29B/2	De Cesaris	4	7. Benetton-Ford		2
7	Patrese	8	Alliot	Lola-Cosworth LC87/01	8. Berger	3	Zakspeed		2
19	Fabi	9	Streiff	Tyrrell-Cosworth DG/016-3	Cheever	3	9. Ligier Megatron		1
2	Johansson	10	Fabre	AGS-Cosworth JH22/02	Nakajima	3			
18	Cheever				11. Boutsen	2			
17	Warwick				Brundle	2			
8	De Cesaris				13. Arnoux	1			
24	Nannini								
11	Nakajima				JIM CLARK CUP		COLIN CHAPMAN CUP		
25	Arnoux				1. Streiff	21	1. Tyrrell-Cosworth		30
26	Ghinzani				2. Alliot	15	2. Lola-Cosworth		15
9	Brundle				3. Fabre	12	3. AGS-Cosworth		12
23	Campos				4. Palmer	9			
10	Danner								
16	Capelli								
30	Alliot								
4	Streiff								
3	Palmer								
14	Fabre								
21	Caffi								

MONACO

31st May 1987
Circuit: Monte Carlo

MONACO. Saturday 30 May. 0700 hours. My hotel room overlooks the harbour and the spectacular 160 mph climb from St Devote to Casino Square. Already the sun is shining brightly from a clear blue sky as a flotilla of millionaires' yachts crowds the shimmering water below. The castellated Royal Palace pierces the skyline. All is calm.

Suddenly, in the overcrowded paddock alongside the palatial floating homes, a Formula One engine bursts harshly into life. Then another, and another, their strident tones rivalling each other — as soon the drivers will be on the track. For this is the day that will decide the starting grid positions for tomorrow's race and who will, therefore, be best placed to win the most glamorous and prestigious Grand Prix of the year.

The man who gets away first at Monaco has a more than sporting chance of staying there for the whole 78 lap, 161 mile, race. The demanding circuit, unique in Grand Prix racing, twists and turns, rises and falls through the streets and around the harbour of the Principality, past the opulent apartments, the five star hotels, the restaurants and the Casino, curving through the frightening 160 mph tunnel under Loews Hotel as it does so. There's nowhere like Monaco. The sponsors, the spectators and the enormous worldwide television audience love it. The drivers and the teams hate it. What is a glorious spectacle for most is a high-pressure misery for the participants. Inadequate temporary scaffolding pits, a ludicrously congested open air paddock and no garages mean awful conditions for the teams. For the drivers virtually nowhere to pass as, for nearly two hours, they constantly brake, accelerate, joust for the best line and change gear some 32 times a lap. All this at speeds of up to 175 mph between solid buildings and endless ribbons of steel Armco barrier. At Monaco they really earn their money.

For years the number of starters allowed at Monaco was sixteen. Then it was raised to twenty and this year to twenty-six — 'to comply with FISA regulations and to bring Monaco into line with the other Grands Prix' (and to avoid distressing the sponsors of non-qualifiers said the cynics!). Not surpri-

Nigel dominated Monaco. Pole position — streets ahead — then no boost. That's motor racing.

singly there were cries of outrage from the faster drivers' teams accompanied by dire prophesies about the catastrophic results of overcrowding, baulking, bunching, the dangers of trying to pass and the speed differentials of the faster and slower cars.

On the first day of practice (Thursday in Monaco) the prophesies seemed all too accurate. In a contentious passing move up the hill to Casino Square Michele Alboreto's Ferrari hit Christian Danner's Zakspeed at some 150 mph. In the colossal accident which ensued the Ferrari was totally destroyed but, miraculously, neither driver was even scratched. Danner, though, was rapidly disqualified from the race to almost universal dismay in a situation where the amiable German was felt to be no more at fault than Alboreto. This, sadly, was the first 'Instant' disqualification in the 37 year history of the World Championships.

Subsequent practice accidents badly damaged the cars of Berger (Ferrari), Fabi (Benetton), Nannini (Minardi), Streiff (Tyrrell) and Campos (Minardi) — more than justifying Monaco's reputation as a car wrecker. However, with the exception of Campos who was not allowed to start as a result of slight concussion, all the drivers were, mercifully, unharmed. 'And you will note' said those same cynics after the exclusion of Campos 'that now the grid is down to 24!'.

At two o'clock on Saturday afternoon the starting grid had been decided . . . to general apprehension. In pole position (and the front row for the fourth successive year) was Nigel Mansell having been as dominant for the whole of the two days' practice as he had been at Spa. Keeping his head down after the unpleasantness of Belgium and simply doing his job of driving he had been in a superlative class of his own. But next to him was his arch rival Ayrton Senna. They had taken each other off in the first lap at Australia '85, Brazil '86 and Belgium '87. Hard and unyielding drivers that they both are would they do so again at St Devote, Monaco's first corner and a traditional danger spot? If they did they'd cause unimaginable carnage behind them.

In the event we needn't have worried. With an absolutely magnificent start Mansell blasted through St Devote with a clear lead over Senna and the rest of the grid led by Piquet, Alboreto, Prost and Cheever. And there he stayed looking absolutely unchallengeable, driving smoothly and precisely until, by lap ten, he had built a commanding eight second cushion between himself and Senna.

For 29 laps the first seven were unchanged. Mansell, Senna, Piquet (still troubled by the after-effects of his massive Imola crash), Alboreto, Prost (with engine problems), Cheever and Berger. But behind them there was action aplenty — not all of it good. On lap six Philippe Streiff had his third massive crash in two weeks. In Belgium the Frenchman had shown that Grand Prix drivers are a very special breed by totally demolishing his Tyrrell and then bravely re-starting, minutes later, in

his spare car (as Alboreto had also done on Thursday at Monaco). In practice Streiff had crashed again and now, in the race, he totalled a third car at the daunting Massenet corner — once again to walk away unharmed. Unharmed but certainly not the flavour of the month with the Tyrrell team!

St Devote too had made its usual first-lap mark when, seconds after the off, both Nakajima and Alliot spun out — the Japanese driver not being able to restart until the others had long since disappeared. He was to drive yet another fine race to tenth place — his fourth finish in as many Grands Prix.

On lap thirty Nigel Mansell's superb drive ended with a broken exhaust primary which caused a loss of turbo boost. Out whilst in the lead for the second race in succession. Bitter luck as past him swept the yellow Lotus-

Jonathan Palmer finished a magnificent fifth in the 'atmospheric' Tyrrell — and scored his first ever Championship points.

Senna's quiet Sunday drive by the sea — first victory for 'Active' suspension Lotus.

Honda of Ayrton Senna. Had Mansell gone too fast too soon? 'Who knows?' said Senna after the race, 'he drove his race and I drove mine. I was determined not to overstress my tyres and when the gap settled at eight seconds with both of us pulling away from the rest I was happy. Monaco is a long race — there was plenty of time to charge when the fuel load had lightened'.

Senna never had to charge though. He stayed in front for the rest of the 48 laps — even when he made a late stop for fresh tyres. Indeed so dominant was he that he made the fastest lap of the race in the closing stages, lap 72, 'just to keep my concentration up'. To say that he was jubilant at winning 'the most important race of them all' would be a masterpiece of understatement. The Lotus people who were on the car-to-pit radio network told me that for the last two laps Senna was positively bubbling with joy inside

his helmet. 'We're going to win this race!' he shouted, 'Easy! Easy! Winning here at Monaco — I can't believe it!'.

Ayrton won by half a minute. A lacklustre Piquet was second after an uneventful but uncomfortable drive — happy enough to finish so well up in the points at Monaco which he doesn't very much like to race at (but lives in!) and to be back in World Championship contention. Third for sixteen glorious laps, to the amazement and delight of the aficionados, was Eddie Cheever driving an inspired race in the Arrows-Megatron chased by Prost's over-heated McLaren, the Ferraris of Alboreto and Berger and Warwick's Arrows — often nose to tail in a blaring, sliding, spectacular Grand Prix crocodile which was a joy to watch.

Just as exciting — sometimes more so — was the progress of Dr Jonathan Palmer's 3½ litre Tyrrell. 'The non-turbos shouldn't be

39

Team Analysis

McLAREN

No joy for McLaren at Monaco. After qualifying disappointed fourth Prost unable to race hard due to overheating engine. Ran third from lap 51 but retired lap 76 (engine). Drivers' Championship lead reduced to three points. Johansson had troubled practice to qualify seventh. Ignition problems during race caused repeated engine cut-outs and retirement lap 58. Down to third in Championship. Failure to score reduces McLaren Constructors' Championship lead to nine points.

TYRRELL

Mixed fortunes for Tyrrell. With the previous misfire at last overcome a superb practice and race for Jonathan Palmer who qualified 15th and finished fifth (first 3½ litre) to achieve first Championship points in 43 race career. Now second in Jim Clark contest, Streiff severely strains Tyrrell relations following Belgian debacle with crashes in practice and race but still leads Jim Clark Trophy. Tyrrell increase lead in Colin Chapman Trophy to 23 points.

WILLIAMS

Race and spare cars for both Mansell and Piquet. Practice dominated by Mansell who achieves third pole position in four races (and seventh of career). Leads dominantly until lap 30 when retires with loss of turbo pressure. Drops to fifth in Championship. Piquet, not fond of Monaco and still unfit after Imola crash, qualifies third and races to second place. Remains fourth in Championship but now only six points behind Prost. Williams, second in Constructors' Championship, narrow McLaren lead to 9 points.

BRABHAM

Troublesome practice with multitude of problems sees Patrese qualify tenth and De Cesaris 21st. Patrese up to eighth by lap 30 but retires lap 42 (electrics). De Cesaris improves to 13th but hits Arnoux Ligier lap 38 and retires with deranged front suspension.

Mansell almost had time to do some shopping.

ZAKSPEED

Practice dominated by grossly unfair 'instant' disqualification of Danner (first-ever in GP history) after major collision with Alboreto. Brundle qualifies 14th despite massive understeer and steadily progresses to despondent seventh at race finish — convincingly beaten by English rival Jonathan Palmer in non-turbo Tyrrell.

Danner before his harsh disqualification.

LOTUS

A magnificent Monaco! Senna qualifies second, calmly follows leader Mansell until his retirement and easily wins untroubled 'most important race of the year'. Senna's fifth win (and fifth fastest lap) in his 50th GP promotes him to second in the Championship. Yet another fine performance by Nakajima to qualify 17th at first Monaco and finish tenth in spite of being blamelessly brought to standstill during first corner incident. First ever 'Active Suspension' GP victory improves Lotus third place Constructors' Championship position.

AGS

Another lacklustre but reliable Grand Prix. Fabre qualifies 24th and last and finishes 13th and last, seven laps down. Consistent finishing puts AGS and Fabre second and third in the two 3½ litre Championships.

MARCH

For first time two superbly presented 1987 cars for the Japanese sponsored English team but many 'new car' problems to overcome in practice. After qualifying 19th Capelli has race-long fight with Jonathan Palmer to finish magnificent sixth (second in class) despite disconnected rev-counter to preserve alternator. Resultant World Championship point for 3½ litre March in only third Grand Prix a fine achievement.

Race 4 — MONACO

ARROWS

A heartbreaking race for the most improved team of 1987. Good practice sees Cheever qualify sixth and Warwick eleventh. Cheever inspired in race running brilliant third for sixteen laps before retiring with waterless engine. After being equally impressive fifth furious Warwick retires (lap 59) for second race running with broken gear linkage. Six championship points lost for Arrows but looking better than ever.

BENETTON

Team arrive lacking confidence in view of worst possible problem at twisty Monaco — major turbo lag. Boutsen nevertheless qualifies surprisingly well (ninth) and is amazing third in Sunday 'warm-up'. Fabi, unhappy on street circuits, destroys race car in Thursday crash caused by oil on circuit. Qualifies 12th in spare. Boutsen retires early (lap six) with broken driveshaft. Fabi finishes praiseworthy eighth two laps down. Ford promise Benetton much-revised engine for Detroit . . .

OSELLA

One of the little Italian team's best-ever meetings — largely thanks to outstanding driving by impressive newcomer Alex Caffi. After qualifying an excellent 16th (in view of the car) he achieved an astounding tenth position by lap 30. Once again, however, unreliability forced retirement on lap 40 (electrics).

MINARDI

Campos not allowed to start after minor concussion caused by Thursday practice accident. Nannini, beset by problems (including three broken driveshafts in half an hour!) qualifies 13th and races consistent twelfth until lap 22 retirement (electrics).

LIGIER

A thoroughly miserable weekend for the Vichy team. Admitting inadequacy of overweight and aerodynamically inefficient car, Designer Michel Tetu returns to base to institute crash programme for new car. Ghinzani and Arnoux qualify disheartening 20th and 22nd. Team mates then collide on lap one to collect broken front aerofoil (Ghinzani) and puncture (Arnoux). After necessary pit work they rejoin to circulate together, finishing 11th (Arnoux) and 12th, four laps down.

Berger's 'flying' practice lap ended up in the air.

FERRARI

Black Thursday for Ferrari. Alboreto destroys car in 150 mph collision with Danner Zakspeed. Berger badly damages monocoque with barrier impact. Rebuilt cars with further suspension and aerodynamic changes qualify fifth (Alboreto) and eighth. Better race, however. Fine Alboreto drive to third with Berger fourth (lapped). Seven points gained improve team's fourth position in Constructors' Championship. Nevertheless rumours that disheartened Alboreto leaving at season end.

LOLA

Car weight now reduced to 512 kg. Alliot qualifies 18th (second 3½ litre) but spins to standstill during lap one St Devote incident with Nakajima and Capelli. Advances to 14th before retiring lap 43 (engine).

*Eddie Cheever was 'inspired'
— but the Arrows broke.*

There is nowhere quite like Monaco.

'Active' suspension even smooths the kerbs.

Stefan's spellbinding high-speed chicanery.

allowed in' almost everybody had said, 'they'll get in the way'. How wrong they were! Palmer, hotly chased by Capelli's March, revelled in the lightness, nimbleness and controllable power of his Tyrrell-Ford V8. Driving magnificently, shaving the Armco but never hitting it, he hurled his car round in complete control making up place after place as the faster turbos wilted. By lap 41 he was eighth (and Capelli ninth). Out went Warwick (gearbox linkage). Out went Cheever (engine). Palmer was in the points at sixth! Then on lap 76 with only two to go out went a philosophical Prost from a gritty third place he'd held, with a sick engine, for 24 laps. 'I suppose I can't complain after three successive wins and I'm still leading the Championship'. Palmer was fifth! Which is where he superbly finished to score his first World Championship points in 43 Grands Prix. An equally impressive Ivan Capelli was sixth to win a Championship point for March which they estimated would save them some $250,000 on travel costs for the year's last three races in Mexico, Japan and Australia! (FOCA points scorers travel free).

A moment's reflection for a Monaco fire marshal.

With Alboreto third, Berger fourth (but lapped) and Martin Brundle a despondent seventh in the turbo Zakspeed, handsomely beaten by his rival Jonathan Palmer in the 3½ litre Tyrrell, it has to be said that the 1987 Monaco Grand Prix was interesting rather than exciting. But it also made history.

Monaco 1987 will be remembered as the first Grand Prix to be won by a car with 'Active'

suspension. Senna's fifth win in his 50th Grand Prix was an historic occasion. 'It isn't right yet' said Lotus 'Active' design genius Peter Wright 'but it's not far off. Detroit should suit us though — it's like Monaco'. And the Detroit Grand Prix was the next . . .

Monaco glitterati — Helen Stewart faces the two number ones.

MONACO GRAND PRIX

Winner: Ayrton Senna, Lotus 99T/4   *Fastest Lap:* Ayrton Senna, 84.918 mph

GRID POSITION		RESULTS		
No.	Driver	Pos.	Driver	Car
5	Mansell	1	Senna	Lotus-Honda 99T/4
12	Senna	2	Piquet	Williams-Honda FW11B/4
6	Piquet	3	Alboreto	Ferrari F187-098
1	Prost	4	Berger	Ferrari F187-095
27	Alboreto	5	Palmer	Tyrrell-Cosworth DG/016-2
18	Cheever	6	Capelli	March-Cosworth 871/01
2	Johansson	7	Brundle	Zakspeed 871/1
28	Berger	8	Fabi	Benetton-Ford B187-04
20	Boutsen	9	Prost	McLaren-TAG MP4/3-3
7	Patrese	10	Nakajima	Lotus-Honda 99T/1
17	Warwick	11	Arnoux	Ligier-Megatron JS29B/3
19	Fabi	12	Ghinzani	Ligier-Megatron JS29B/2
24	Nannini	13	Fabre	AGS-Cosworth JH22/02
9	Brundle			
3	Palmer			
21	Caffi			
11	Nakajima			
30	Alliot			
16	Capelli			
26	Ghinzani			
8	De Cesaris			
25	Arnoux			
4	Streiff			
14	Fabre			

WORLD CHAMPIONSHIP				
Drivers	Pts	Constructors	Pts	
1. Prost	18	1. McLaren-TAG	31	
2. Senna	15	2. Williams-Honda	22	
3. Johansson	13	3. Lotus-Honda	18	
4. Piquet	12	4. Ferrari	14	
5. Mansell	10	5. Brabham-BMW	4	
6. Alboreto	8	6. Arrows-Megatron	3	
7. Berger	6	7. Benetton-Ford	2	
8. De Cesaris	4	Tyrrell-Cosworth	2	
9. Cheever	3	Zakspeed	2	
Nakajima	3	10. Ligier-Megatron	1	
11. Boutsen	2	March-Cosworth	1	
Brundle	2			
Palmer	2			
14. Arnoux	1			
Capelli	1			

JIM CLARK CUP		COLIN CHAPMAN CUP		
1. Streiff	21	1. Tyrrell-Cosworth	39	
2. Palmer	18	2. AGS-Cosworth	16	
3. Fabre	16	3. Lola-Cosworth	15	
4. Alliot	15	4. March-Cosworth	6	
5. Capelli	6			

USA EAST

21st June 1987
Circuit: Detroit

AYRTON SENNA does not suffer fools gladly. 'Why didn't you change tyres?' a journalist aggressively asked him after the race. 'Because it wasn't necesssary' came the terse reply. And those five words summed up why Senna brilliantly won both his second successive 1987 Grand Prix and his second successive race at Detroit.

Until lap thirty-four out of sixty-three Detroit had been Nigel Mansell's meeting. In crushingly dominant form he had been fastest in both the qualifying practice sessions to take his fourth pole position of the season just over one second faster than his nearest rival who, almost needless to say, was Senna. One second is light years at Detroit. In the final Sunday morning half hour practice Mansell was fastest again and when the lights turned to green he made a perfect start. At the end of the lap he led Senna by a clear ten lengths. By lap ten it was five seconds and on lap 25 it was twenty seconds. Mansell had the race winning cushion he needed. Monaco repeated!

On lap 33 he shot into the pit lane for the tyre stop that was a major factor in his race defeat — and Senna's victory. For, as is Nigel's Williams mechanics struggled with a jammed right rear wheel nut which extended his stop to nineteen seconds instead of the usual eight, Senna took the lead he was never to lose.

Ayrton's win was a blend of superior driving, tactics and machinery. Early in the race the Brazilian had brake problems similar to those which had resulted in him ending up in the wall in 1985. So, with a secure second place, he wisely backed off. In doing so he gave his Goodyears an easier time and, at his planned tyre stop, opted to drive on and see how things developed. When he got the message over his pits-to-car radio that Mansell's tyres had looked good enough to go the whole distance Senna decided to stay out with the knowledge that he only had to keep going at what, for him, was an easy pace to win the race. Which he did — with race and lap

records. As at Monaco so at Detroit the combination of Senna's brains and driving ability, Honda power and the 'Active' suspension of the superb Lotus 99T ensured a richly deserved 79th Grand Prix victory for the Hethel Team.

No one likes Detroit. There are no proper pits and no garages. Being a street circuit it is impossible to test there. The heat, the humidity, the repeated gear changing and braking for almost two hours, the need for total and unremitting concentration, the bumpiness and the ever-present walls make dangerously exhausting demands on both the drivers and the cars.

The statues are big in Detroit. The room for error is not.

Racing at Detroit is a perpetual battle to 'stay on the Island' driving at an AVERAGE of 85 mph writhing around concrete walls where even a millimetre deviation from the correct line can take you out of the race. In practice alone Patrese, De Cesaris, Brundle, Nakajima, Fabi, Campos and Berger had car damaging accidents of varying severity. Nobody disagreed with the sensible and temperate Alain Prost when he said, 'I hate it here. The track is a joke. We race here simply because it's in America where everyone says we must race. I agree with that but this place gives Americans no idea of what Formular One is really like. There are some great tracks here — Watkins Glen for instance. Why don't we use one of them and make everybody happy?' The answer is a mixture of status, prestige and commercialism. Detroit is 'Motor City USA' and the Industry's 'Top Brass' want to watch an American Grand Prix there. Especially this year; General Motors to see 'their' 'Active' suspension (GM own Lotus) in action and Ford to see how the Benettons would go with their much improved V6 turbos. And whether any of the Ford 3½ litre powered cars would benefit enough from the street circuit 'point and squirt' needs of Detroit to finish well up in the points. GM were to be delighted and Ford disappointed.

Practice, in ninety degree heat and similar humidity, had seen a mixed bag of achievements: The organisers fined $20,000 by FISA for starting the first session late. Mansell and Senna sharing the front row of the grid for the third time in five races, Piquet, who (despite winning there in 1984) dislikes Detroit almost as much as Prost, taking third place, and Boutsen, revelling in the almost total lack of turbo-lag from his Benetton's revised Ford engine, occupying his highest ever grid position — fourth — ahead of resigned Prost and a very satisfied Eddie Cheever.

McLaren won the first Detroit Grand Prix in 1982 with an inspired drive by John Watson but since then they've never done well there. This year both Prost and Johansson were so bedevilled by the general complaint — no grip — that they qualified with some 150 litres of fuel aboard, incurring a performance-sapping weight penalty in the process. The McLaren view was that this was going to be a Williams and Lotus benefit. They were right!

The race was a mixture of incidents and attrition — behind Mansell and Senna there was incident aplenty. On lap 33 Piquet, in third place, collected a front puncture whilst striving to fend off Eddie Cheever who had charged up from sixth on the grid to fourth past Prost and Boutsen. Restarting in twenty-first place with new rubber, Nelson drove one of the finest races of his 130 Grands Prix career. By lap 26 he was sixth and in the points. On lap 53 he had the supreme satisfaction of being waved by into second place by his arch-rival 'team mate' Nigel Mansell. A place he held to the end. Nigel's progress seemed strangely erratic. After breaking the lap record immediately following his tyre stop his driving became visibly jerky and his lap times variable. The reason became clear only at the end of the race. Having progressively slipped down the order to fifth place he had to be lifted from the car in a state of dehydrated exhaustion and with agonising cramp in his right leg. If the super-fit Mansell had suffered what about the others? They were mostly in a similar state with one notable exception — the 'Actively' suspended Senna who, comparatively fresh and with no hand blisters, was in significantly better shape than both Piquet and Prost as he jubilantly sprayed the champagne. The Lotus innovation clearly benefits the driver as well as the tyres.

So Lotus number two Nakajima must have been in good physical condition too? Yes he was but for quite the wrong reason. For Satoru, excitedly accompanied by his camera car by TV's viewing millions, comprehensively blotted his proud 100%-finish GP record by involving himself in two separate incidents from his twenty-fourth grid position. A collision with Capelli on the first lap immediately followed by another with Adrian Campos which took the Lotus number two and the Spaniard back to the Westin Hotel for an early bath.

Up front, as Piquet drove the field on the one set of tyres he'd collected on lap three (to show that Mansell, like Senna, could have

---

Suspended 'Active' suspension. Testing it this way was not Ayrton's choice!

Team Analysis

McLAREN

Expected comparative lack of success (by their high standards). MP4 chassis does not suit Detroit. Fifth on grid for Prost ('no grip') who detests circuit, has brake and gearbox problems and is happy to finish third. Down to unconcerned second in Championship. Johansson qualifies lowly eleventh ('no grip!'). First lap collision damages front wing. Subsequent misfire requires stop for new Motronic box. Finishes seventh (three laps down) and drops to fourth in Championship. McLaren still lead Constructors' Championship but by reduced margin of five points over Williams.

TYRRELL

Street circuit high hopes for nimble instant-response, 3½ litre cars (with new Courtaulds livery) only partially realised. Palmer in top form all meeting. Thirteenth (top 3½ litre) on grid and eleventh in race three laps down despite remedial pit stop after blameless contact with Patrese Brabham. With 3½ litre win takes lead for Jim Clark Trophy. Streiff, fully recovered from Monaco cracked ribs, qualifies fourteenth and races to excellent sixth until rear wheel departs scene lap 45. Down to third in Jim Clark Trophy. Tyrrell, only two-car 3½ litre team, extend Colin Chapman Trophy lead to 26 points.

WILLIAMS

A good but 'could-have-been-much-better' race. Three cars with revised Honda engines. 'Streetfighter' Mansell again dominates practice to take fourth pole position in five races. Leads race commandingly until lap 33 tyre stop. Thereafter slides to lapped fifth with lack of grip, brake problems and cramp-induced exhaustion. Still fifth in Championship — twelve points behind leader. Piquet qualifies third and drives from 21st to inspired second after puncture. Moves up Championship place to third. Team still second to McLaren in Constructors' contest.

BRABHAM

Team going through bad patch. Designer David North and Engineer John Gentry leave after Monaco. Patrese qualifies and finishes ninth (three laps down) after clouting Palmer's Tyrrell and several stops with defective harness. 'De Crasheris' increases unpopularity with team by shunting twice in practice and destroying gearbox on lap two.

ZAKSPEED

Revised, improved response, engine. Unhappy practice for Brundle. Engine fire on Friday and shunt on Saturday. Fifteenth on grid. Races spare car to retire lap seventeen with turbo fire. Welcome return by Danner after harsh Monaco exclusion. Steady and encouraging race improving from grid sixteenth to finish eighth.

LOTUS

Another excellent GP win (their 79th) for Hethel team who follow Active Suspension innovation with first time GP use of 5½" Tilton carbon-fibre clutch (improves engine response/

No exit problems for Nigel in practice — after the race he had to be lifted out.

speeds gearchanges). Revised Honda engines and rear wing/undertray modifications to increase downforce. After qualifying second Senna drives superb non-stop tactical race overcoming brake problems to win second successive victory (in 1987 and at Detroit) with race and lap records. Now leads World Championship. Nakajima comprehensively destroys '100% finish' record with two separate first lap collisions (Capelli and Campos) after unhappy 24th place on grid. With second 'Active' suspension win Team Lotus now only eight points behind Constructors' Championship leader, McLaren.

AGS

Fabre qualifies 26th and last. Finishes twelfth and last, five laps down. Nevertheless AGS reliability (100% finish record) moves Fabre up to second in 3½ litre Drivers' Championship and retains second in Constructors' contest.

MARCH

First-time-at-Detroit problems for both team and driver. Capelli, 22nd on grid after overheating problems, assaulted by Nakajima Lotus lap one and stopped by electrical failure on lap nine.

ARROWS

A 'Curate's Egg' race on enthusiastic sponsor's (USF&G) home ground. Another disastrous weekend for Warwick. Sick on Friday. Engine failure on Saturday. Tenth on grid. Retires lap 12 after wall-induced suspension damage when eighth.

Still no points. Another outstanding meeting for Cheever, Sixth on grid and running third until thumped by Fabi Benetton lap seven. After pit stop recovers magnificently from 21st to sixth. Arrows advance to fifth in Constructors' Championship having already scored four times as many points as in the whole of 1986!

BENETTON

Previous Ford engine response problem totally overcome by revised turbo and electronics. Fabi drives spare car from eighth on grid after damaging race car in practice. Harpoons third place Cheever lap seven and retires following pit crew inability to fit replacement nose cone. Boutsen, delighted with revised engine, starts excellent fourth but, after wrestling with gear selection and brake problems, retires on lap 53. Ford Top Brass had hoped for better . . .

OSELLA

The hard-trying underfinanced Osella team thought they'd seen it all but they hadn't. A new, character-building, failure at Detroit when, after qualifying 19th (way above expectations) Caffi retires on lap four with — a broken gear lever!

MINARDI

Like Osella another disheartening race for Minardi. Adrian Campos, adding to the strong general belief that he is not yet ready for Formula One, follows Monaco practice crash with another at Detroit. Instant retirement after lap one race collision with Nakajima. Alessandro Nannini again impresses. Tenth in Friday practice but 18th on grid after Saturday gearbox problems which recur to take him out of race (lap 22) when an excellent eleventh. But another promising meeting that the talent scouts have noted . . .

> *26 started — 12 finished. Not bad for Detroit!*

LIGIER

Post-Monaco work in St Cyr wind tunnel produces revised radiator inlets but lack of time precludes other vital design changes. Arnoux qualifies 21st ('no grip') and finishes tenth, three laps down, after terminating countryman Alliot's race against barrier. Ghinzani 23rd on grid (electrical gremlins), retires lap 52 with inoperative clutch. Re-work of cars continues at furious pace for next vital race — the home ground French Grand Prix.

FERRARI

Getting closer but not close enough. Improved engine response and experiments with Gleason differential and 7½" carbon-fibre clutch (Lotus has exclusive on 5½"). Alboreto qualifies seventh and races promising third (laps 7-24). Retires lap 26 (gearbox). Ends 'moving in 1988' speculation by re-signing with Ferrari. Berger qualifies twelfth with handling problems. Finishes strong fourth (last to go full 63 laps) and improves to sixth in Championship. Team retain Constructors' Championship fourth place but with increased gap.

LOLA

Team Principal Gerard Larrousse's hopes for good finish with circuit-suiting 3½ litre Lola-Ford unfulfilled. Alliot starts 20th and impressively improves to eleventh only to end race in wall after unsuccessfully trying to pass unyielding Arnoux.

> *Ford power in Detroit didn't help Fabi — he crashed.*

gone through non-stop) Cheever and Teo Fabi were now battling for the third place that Nelson had lost. But not for long! Attempting an impossible passing manoeuvre Fabi harpooned the American's Arrows to force 'Fast Eddie' into the pits with a right rear puncture whilst Teo retired when his Benetton mechanics were unable to make a replacement nose cone fit.

Cheever then 'did a Piquet', remorselessly progressing from nineteenth on lap seven to sixth on lap forty-four. And there he stayed although, after brilliant drives at Monaco and Detroit, it was clear that if only he could finish

Too easy for Senna? He drove a brilliant race on just one set of tyres.

Don't worry Nelson, you won't always finish second.

a race without problems he was going to be where he deserved to be — at the front. But alas poor Warwick, Eddie's team mate, once again failed to finish. This time with a severely deranged rear suspension after clouting the concrete on lap twelve when he was in a strong eighth place.

Further ahead the World Champion, Alain Prost, was tigering on in a car which was far from right for the conditions but of which he was making the best, as ever. Briefly second he finished a well-pleased third. 'Third for me at Detroit is like winning,' he said. 'I'm still second in the Championship and with Monaco and Detroit behind me the Championship starts now! With the fast circuits coming up McLaren is the car to have. I am happy'. Which is more than Stefan Johansson was. For, after finishing seventh and out of the points in a race where he had to stop for a new McLaren nose cone after hitting Warwick, plus a new Motronic electronics box to rectify a misfire, he was now down to fourth in the Championship.

But what about Ferrari — and the 3½ litre cars?

Alboreto, third at San Marino and Monaco, was third at Detroit for eighteen laps and looking good for another place on the podium. Until lap 25 when, leading Prost, Berger and Boutsen, his gearbox called it a day. Berger started twelfth (after going off in practice) and finished fourth for the third time (Brazil, Monaco and Detroit) after a trouble free race. Except that his Ferrari still wasn't fast enough.

The 3½ litre cars disappointed their fans at Detroit. After their fifth and sixth places at Monaco (Palmer and Capelli) they were expected to go even better at Motown with their benefits of instant response, nimbleness and no hill to disadvantage them. Jonathan Palmer led the class in eleventh place until being savaged by Patrese's Brabham on lap six. Team mate Philippe Streiff then took over to climb to a fine sixth, points scoring, place on lap 43 — only to lose a rear wheel and let the delighted Palmer back into a class winning place, eleventh overall.

Only four men went the distance at Detroit. Senna, Piquet, Prost and Berger. Senna now led the Drivers' Championship after two brilliant victories on the two slowest and bumpiest circuits where the Lotus 'Active' suspension would benefit him most. How would he go on the fast tracks which followed? With the near 120 mph French Grand Prix in two weeks' time we'd soon know!

René Arnoux. Ligier JS29B — he finished tenth.

'Show me the way to go home' — Ferraris in line.

USA EAST GRAND PRIX

Winner: Ayrton Senna, Lotus 99T/4   **Fastest Lap:** Ayrton Senna, 89.584 mph

GRID POSITION		RESULTS			WORLD CHAMPIONSHIP				
No.	Driver	Pos.	Driver	Car	Drivers	Pts	Constructors		Pts
5	Mansell	1	Senna	Lotus-Honda 99T/4	1. Senna	24	1. McLaren-TAG		35
12	Senna	2	Piquet	Williams-Honda FW11B/4	2. Prost	22	2. Williams-Honda		30
6	Piquet	3	Prost	McLaren-TAG MP4/2C-3	3. Piquet	18	3. Lotus-Honda		27
20	Boutsen	4	Berger	Ferrari F187-095	4. Johansson	13	4. Ferrari		17
1	Prost	5	Mansell	Williams-Honda FW11B/3	5. Mansell	12	5. Arrows-Megatron		4
18	Cheever	6	Cheever	Arrows-Megatron MP4/2C-2	6. Berger	9	Brabham-BMW		4
27	Alboreto	7	Johansson	McLaren-TAG MP4/2C-2	7. Alboreto	8	7. Benetton-Ford		2
19	Fabi	8	Danner	Zakspeed 871/2	8. Cheever	4	Tyrrell-Cosworth		2
7	Patrese	9	Patrese	Brabham-BMW BT56/3	De Cesaris	4	Zakspeed		2
17	Warwick	10	Arnoux	Ligier-Megatron JS29B/4	10. Nakajima	3	10. Ligier-Megatron		1
2	Johansson	11	Palmer	Tyrrell-Cosworth DG/016-3	11. Boutsen	2	March-Cosworth		1
28	Berger	12	Fabre	AGS-Cosworth JH22/02	Brundle	2			
3	Palmer				Palmer	2			
4	Streiff				14. Arnoux	1			
9	Brundle				Capelli	1			
10	Danner								
8	De Cesaris				**JIM CLARK CUP**		**COLIN CHAPMAN CUP**		
24	Nannini				1. Palmer	27	1. Tyrrell-Cosworth		48
21	Caffi				2. Fabre	22	2. AGS-Cosworth		22
30	Alliot				3. Streiff	21	3. Lola-Cosworth		15
25	Arnoux				4. Alliot	15	4. March-Cosworth		6
16	Capelli				5. Capelli	6			
26	Ghinzani								
11	Nakajima								
23	Campos								
14	Fabre								

FRANCE

5th July 1987
Circuit: Paul Ricard

LIFE for a Grand Prix driver is full of ups and downs. Nigel Mansell had had his share of downs in the six weeks preceding his trip to France for round six of the World Championship. Pole position in the last three races but only two Championship points. Bad publicity after his Belgian assault on Senna. Victory snatched from his grasp at Monaco — and then again at Detroit.

Now he was only fifth in the Championship with half the points of the leader, Ayrton Senna. Time to get it all together! And Nigel, never short of gritty determination, did just that.

Over the two days of practice in the exhausting 100 degree heat at the Paul Ricard circuit he was simply awe-inspiring, dominating the proceedings even more than he had in Belgium, Monaco and Detroit. Fastest in all four sessions on Friday and Saturday (and in the Sunday morning 'warm-up') he took his fifth pole position from six races and, what is more, did so with a time faster than Senna's 1986 pole despite the limitations of reduced turbo boost and race tyres. But, even more significantly, he did so early enough to get in a lot of extra full-tank running to study fuel consumption and tyre wear — critical factors at Paul Ricard.

After thankfully saying goodbye to the unloved street circuits at Monaco and Detroit the teams were looking forward to getting back to 'real' racing involving sheer speed. Before them lay three of the quick ones — France, Silverstone and Hockenheim, so it was with relief and enthusiasm that they assembled on the Cote d'Azur.

The Paul Ricard circuit, named after the Pastis manufacturer who built and owns it, is about half an hour's motoring north of Toulon on a high, fir-clad, rocky plateau ringed with barren mountains. It is flat, 2.4 miles long and fast, 210 miles an hour on the wide Mistral Straight and a lap speed of nearly 125 mph. The flat out right hander at Signes and the seemingly endless double right at Beausset which is taken at some 140 mph, put terrific stress on the two left tyres. The race of 80 laps; 190 miles, at an average speed of well over 115 mph with a maximum fuel allowance of 195 litres makes great demands on engine fuel efficiency. So Mansell's extra testing time gave him a bonus he was to use to great effect.

Practice produced a surprise. For the first time since Mexico 1986 a car without Honda power occupied a starting grid front row position — Prost's McLaren-TAG. Neither Alain nor the team usually excercise themselves too much about pole position during practice preferring to concentrate on getting the best race set-up. But both the car and the driver revel in fast circuits and, for the start of his home GP, the Frenchman faced a clear track alongside Mansell. Senna third, Piquet fourth, the Benettons of Boutsen and Fabi fifth and seventh, sandwiching Berger's Ferrari, and Alboreto (Ferrari) eighth. Nothing unusual about that. But, after their greater competitiveness on the twisty street circuits, the 3½ litre cars were outclassed in France. Ivan Capelli's March, 22nd on the grid, was the best with a lap time over six seconds off the pace and with a speed deficiency of nearly 30 mph on the Mistral Straight.

When starter Roland Bruynseraede lit the green the Ferraris blew it. Alboreto was already on his way — for which he incurred a sixty-second penalty. Berger averaged out the Maranello cars' starts by staying where he was!

Mansell shot away first. Prost's start-line advantage didn't last long as Piquet, having

Pascal Fabre in his AGS Cosworth — he finished last but maintained his 100% finishing record.

No-one expected the 'atmospheric' Tyrrells to do well at the Paul Ricard 'power' circuit. But Streiff was a superb sixth (and Palmer seventh).

already taken Senna, blasted past him on the Mistral Straight and when Alain's team-mate Stefan Johansson arrived at the first corner and had his McLaren nosecone rudely trodden on by Andrea de Cesaris making one of his tunnel-vision charges, the fortunes of the red and white cars looked dubious.

Lap one: Mansell, Piquet, Prost, Senna, Boutsen, Fabi, Patrese and De Cesaris. Already the Williams-Hondas were in charge but the Benettons with their further modified Ford engines were right up with the action. Eddie Cheever wasn't though! On the very first lap, reaching for the turbo boost button to improve on his fourteenth place on the grid he set off the fire extinguisher. A humiliating way to end his French Grand Prix.

As Eddie despondently trudged back to his pit millions of TV viewers around the world were increasingly enthralled by a thrilling battle for the lead. Mansell, Piquet and Prost drove around Paul Ricard covered by a mere two seconds each watching the other — and watching their read-out counters to make sure they weren't using too much fuel.

Lap nineteen. Piquet half-spins to give Prost the opportunity he'd been patiently waiting for. Through to second went the McLaren. Down to third went Piquet with Senna now some fifteen seconds back in fourth place and seemingly out of contention. Before the race Lotus had said they weren't over-optimistic about winning in France. It was looking as though they were right.

Lap thirty. With under three seconds covering Mansell, Prost and Piquet into the pit lane shot Nelson for a change of tyres — 9.6 seconds. Good but not brilliant these days. Back into the race, now fifth behind Senna and Boutsen.

Lap thirty-two. Senna in for tyres. Boutsen out of the race (electrics) to join the other retirees — Cheever, De Cesaris, Brundle

(wheel off after his tyre stop!), Patrese, Danner, Caffi, Nannini and Ghinzani. Seventeen left out of twenty-six starters with Ivan Capelli (March) leading the 3½ litre class in a magnificent tenth place.

Piquet back to third behind Mansell and Prost. But on lap 36, with both Mansell and Prost in for tyres, Nelson took the lead. Was he going to win his first Grand Prix of 1987? Not if Mansell could help it! With no team orders and with barely concealed dislike between them it was every man for himself as far as the two Williams drivers were concerned.

Rapidly disposing of Prost as they lapped the mid-field men Mansell closed on Piquet with fastest lap after fastest lap. On lap 45 he was under the Brazilian's rear wing. Lap 46 and

When the light turned to green, it all went wrong for Ferrari. Berger stalled. Behind him Alboreto was penalised for jumping the start. Neither finished.

Team Analysis

McLAREN

Overall results not up to expectations at circuit car suits. Prost achieves first 1987 front row grid position (2nd). Races third behind Mansell/Piquet for virtually whole 80 laps. Performance adversely affected by electronic and gearbox problems. Finishes third. Retains Championship second place. Johansson again qualifies badly (9th). Two separate pit stops for new nosecone and front wing but recovers magnificiently to sixth before lap 75 retirement (alternator belt). Drops to fifth in Championship. McLaren loses Constructors Championship lead to Williams.

TYRRELL

Fast circuit prospects viewed with gloom. Lack of straight line speed confirms pessimism in practice but superb race result. Palmer 24th on grid. Steadily improves to finish seventh overall (second in class) four laps down. Retains Class Championship lead. Streiff qualifies 25th but excellent race in home GP to finish sixth overall for first 1987 Championship point. Now second in Jim Clark Trophy contest. First and second in class massively increases team's lead in 3½ litre Constructors Championship.

Brundle's Zakspeed looks as if it's only got three wheels — and that's how it ended the race.

The Campos Minardi looked good but just wasn't competitive.

WILLIAMS

Cars ideally suited to Paul Ricard circuit. Mansell dominates meeting. Fastest in all five practice sessions. Fifth pole position from six 1987 races. Pole faster than 1986 despite lower boost and race tyres. Brilliantly leads race for 70 out of 80 laps to take second win of season. Up to fourth in Championship and now only six points behind leader. Piquet, agitating about alleged unequal treatment by team, qualifies fourth. Loses second place to Prost for eighteen laps after half-spin. Leads for ten laps following Mansell tyre stop but loses chance to challenge for victory by stopping for second set of tyres. Fifteen points for first two places gives team Constructors Championship lead.

BRABHAM

John Baldwin now in charge of team. Aerodynamic changes to car since Detroit. Riccardo Patrese's 150th Grand Prix. Qualifies twelfth. Races to seventh by lap thirteen. Retires lap 20 (turbo). De Cesaris eleventh on grid. Retires lap three (spectacular turbo fire).

ZAKSPEED

Three 1987 cars at meeting for first time. Brundle starts 18th in spare car after warm-up misfire. Hard charges to 13th on first lap. Retires lap 19 when faultily fitted rear wheel leaves car after tyre stop. Danner 19th on grid, improves to tenth (lap 12). Retires lap 27 with turbo failure.

LOTUS

Substantial aerodynamic modifications for fast circuits following two days in St Cyr (Paris) wind tunnel. Senna qualifies third and runs steady fourth to end of race ('No car problem. I couldn't keep up'). Still leads Championship but now only one point ahead of Prost. Character-building race for Nakajima. First time at Paul Ricard. Qualifies 16th. Pits three times (rear puncture-nosecone/front brake shroud). Completes 71 laps in last place. Team Lotus retain Constructors Championship third place but with increased gap.

56

AGS

Enthusiastic twelve man team acknowledge car 70kg overweight and 'too long' (based on 1984 Renault body moulds). Nevertheless Pascal Fabre again keeps going to finish ninth, four laps down, and retain 100% finish record. Team and driver respectively second and third in class championships.

MARCH

Race car falls off jack in garage and writes off carbon fibre monocoque. Capelli qualifies 22nd and fastest 3½ litre. Races to and holds inspired ninth (and class leadership) until lap 50. Retires lap 53 (engine) having again emphasised his outstanding ability.

ARROWS

Bad race for the team. Warwick qualifies strong tenth and progresses to eighth before retiring lap 63 (turbo). Has yet to finish 1987 race. Almost instant lap one retirement for Cheever who inadvertently activates fire extinguisher instead of turbo boost after starting 14th.

BENETTON

After promising Silverstone test following suspension changes and further modifications to Ford Turbo engine another disappointing meeting for hard-trying team. Repeated engine and turbo failures during practice. Cars unknown quantity for race. Nevertheless, Fabi achieves second 1987 finish (despite a puncture and broken driveshaft) three laps down in fifth place to score first points of year after starting seventh. Boutsen starts and races fifth until lap 31 retirement (electrics).

Electrical failure robbed Boutsen of points.

OSELLA

Usual fraught practice with various unreliability problems. Capable Alex Caffi qualifies 20th despite limited running. Retires from 24th and last place on lap twelve (gearbox).

Alliot's Lola — 'beautifully prepared'.

MINARDI

Campos collides with Johansson Friday a.m. practice. Starts 21st. Benefits from retirements to 14th place. Retires lap 53 (turbo). Nannini qualifies well at 15th but retires from eleventh lap 24 (engine failure).

LIGIER

Crash programme to revise car following change to Megatron engine yields results. Lighter by 25kg. Altered radiators and aerodynamics. Encouraging testing at Hockenheim. Major concern over fuel consumption remains. Arnoux starts 13th. Progresses to eighth, lap 14. Slides out of contention with long pit stop (collapsed exhaust). Retires lap 34. Ghinzani qualifies 17th. Races spare car after problems in warm-up. Retires from eleventh, on lap 25.

FERRARI

Further invisible changes to engine (improved response), suspension, aerodynamics and gearbox but both drivers complain of massive understeer. General management complaints about 'time Barnard taking to get things right' whilst he doggedly soldiers on in hostile atmosphere. Both drivers sign 1988 one-year contracts. Alboreto eighth on grid. Penalised 60 seconds for jumping start. Retires from sixth lap 65 — plus penalty — (engine). Berger muffs start from sixth on grid. Improves from 19th lap one to fifth lap 36. Retires from ninth lap 72 after lengthy pit stop (suspension) Ferrari retain Constructors Championship fourth place 28 points behind Williams.

LOLA

Philippe Alliot qualifies 23rd in usual beautifully prepared car. Races impressively in twelfth place laps 30-57. Retires lap 58 (ignition failure).

as Nelson ran slightly wide at Beausset Mansell brilliantly dived inside him to exit the corner back in the lead. A lead he never lost.

The night before the race Mansell had had a long telephone conversation with Williams designer Patrick Head who was sitting this one out in England. Armed with the results of those fruitful practice full tank tests they discussed race tactics. Should Nigel go for one tyre stop or two — as he had on his way to winning the 1986 race? One, they decided — provided he could get to lap 35 without having to stop. He did.

But Piquet, right up with Mansell, thought differently. On lap 65 he made a second, disastrous, stop, stalling his engine to double the usual eight second delay. 'I didn't stall it,' he said afterwards, 'it stopped!' Whatever the reason that extra eight seconds cost Piquet any chance he might have had to beat Mansell. Rejoining at lap-record breaking speed he caught and passed Prost on lap 67 with a gap now of some twenty seconds between himself and Mansell.

As Prost fell back with a power-sapping electrical problem which also affected his ability to change gear cleanly Nelson gained on Mansell at some two seconds a lap. He had been complaining for some time about what he believed to be unequal treatment by his team and now he was going to show them who was best! With seven laps to go the gap was thirteen seconds but there it stayed until Mansell, pacing himself to victory, crossed the line to win by 7.7 seconds. If Nelson hadn't lost those eight seconds . . .

With Prost third and last to go the full distance Senna was fourth but lapped. Fabi was fifth, three laps down, followed by a euphoric Philippe Streiff finishing sixth overall after a fine drive to take his first 1987 World Championship point and win the 3½ Litre class. In fact, with Jonathan Palmer seventh it was an unexpectedly excellent day for Ken Tyrrell's team.

Once again it was Nigel Mansell's day and now, with the British Grand Prix at Silverstone in a week's time, he was fourth in the

Patrese and Arnoux in battle.

Human power for Nigel after car weight check.

Riccardo 'Iceberg cool' in hot French sun.

Championship only six points behind the leader, Ayrton Senna. The Williams team, now leading the Constructors Championship thanks to their fifteen points from France, were happy indeed. But for the other front runners it was a mostly worrying day. McLaren had been soundly beaten and had seen poor Johansson fight back from last to sixth after two stops to remedy contact damage only to retire with five laps to go. Lotus, in effect a one-man team, had seen Senna unable to keep up in spite of the fact that his car was sound — 'just not fast enough' — Ferrari had failed to finish either car and now looked back over a 29 race gap to their last win. And, at a circuit where they had hoped to do much better, Benetton had again failed to realise their potential.

Mansell and Wiliams had indeed got it all together. Could the others do the same in less than a week?

Mansell dominated Ricard.

FRENCH GRAND PRIX

Winner: Nigel Mansell, Williams FW11B/3   *Fastest Lap:* Nelson Piquet, 122.811 mph

GRID POSITION		RESULTS		
No.	Driver	Pos.	Driver	Car
5	Mansell	1	Mansell	Williams-Honda FW11B/3
1	Prost	2	Piquet	Williams-Honda FW11B/4
12	Senna	3	Prost	McLaren-TAG MP4/3C-3
6	Piquet	4	Senna	Lotus-Honda 99T/4
20	Boutsen	5	Fabi	Benetton-Ford B187-04
28	Berger	6	Streiff	Tyrrell-Cosworth DG/016-5
19	Fabi	7	Palmer	Tyrrell-Cosworth DG/016-2
27	Alboreto	8	Johansson	McLaren-TAG MP4/3C-2
2	Johansson	9	Fabre	AGS-Cosworth JH22/02
17	Warwick			
8	De Cesaris			
7	Patrese			
25	Arnoux			
18	Cheever			
24	Nannini			
11	Nakajima			
26	Ghinzani			
9	Brundle			
10	Danner			
21	Caffi			
23	Campos			
16	Capelli			
30	Alliot			
3	Palmer			
4	Streiff			
14	Fabre			

WORLD CHAMPIONSHIP

Drivers	Pts	Constructors	Pts
1. Senna	27	1. Williams-Honda	45
2. Prost	26	2. McLaren-TAG	39
3. Piquet	24	3. Lotus-Honda	30
4. Mansell	21	4. Ferrari	17
5. Johansson	13	5. Arrows-Megatron	4
6. Berger	9	Benetton-Ford	4
7. Alboreto	8	Brabham-BMW	4
8. Cheever	4	8. Tyrrell-Cosworth	3
De Cesaris	4	9. Zakspeed	2
10. Nakajima	3	10. Ligier-Megatron	1
11. Boutsen	2	March Cosworth	1
Brundle	2		
Fabi	2		
Palmer	2		
15. Arnoux	1		
Capelli	1		
Streiff	1		

JIM CLARK CUP

	Pts
1. Palmer	33
2. Streiff	30
3. Fabre	26
4. Alliot	15
5. Capelli	6

COLIN CHAPMAN CUP

	Pts
1. Tyrrell-Cosworth	63
2. AGS-Cosworth	26
3. Lola-Cosworth	15
4. March-Cosworth	6

GREAT BRITAIN

12th July 1987
Circuit: Silverstone

NIGEL MANSELL, making a lap of honour on the pillion of a Police BMW motorcycle, motioned his 'Chauffeur' to stop at Stowe Corner. Still in his decal-covered, sweat soaked, racing overalls he got off, knelt down and kissed the ground. For this was the spot where he had audaciously passed his team-mate Nelson Piquet to take the lead and win his second successive British Grand Prix. On lap 63 out of 65. In what was undoubtedly the finest race of his career.

The enthusiastic and knowledgeable crowd loved it — as well they might. The record 100,000 plus who had poured into Silverstone had spent the last twenty laps of the race literally willing Mansell to victory. Shouting, cheering, waving flags and programmes as he masterfully sliced second after second off Piquet's lead — repeatedly breaking the lap record to eliminate a 28 second deficit caused by an unplanned tyre stop and then go on to win by a mere 1.9 seconds.

Ten laps after the race began and in a comfortable second place behind Piquet, who had started from his first pole position of 1987, Mansell's Williams was vibrating so much as the result of the left front wheel balance weight detaching itself from its wheel rim that 'I couldn't see the next corner properly and could hardly hang on to Nelson'. So, on lap 35, with 30 still to go Nigel stopped for a new set of balanced wheels and Goodyear 'boots' whilst Piquet, now in a race of his own, drove non-stop to what seemed an unchallengeable first win of the year. Just 9.1 seconds after he'd arrived at the pit, Mansell left — another brilliant Williams team demonstration of wheel changing under extreme pressure.

Throwing caution to the winds he charged. Ignoring his fuel counter and never putting a wheel wrong he brilliantly caught and took Piquet with only two laps to go feinting to his left, Piquet covered him, only to find Mansell

How not to take pole from Piquet — Mansell tries too hard.

screaming past inside. With failing grip from worn tyres the Brazilian was powerless to respond. The vast crowd had come to Silverstone to see their hero win and he'd made their dream come true. Even to the extent of running out of fuel amongst them as they happily invaded the track on his run-down lap!

In Grand Prix racing, as in life, you need to be lucky as well as good if you're to succeed. At Silverstone Nigel was lucky to win just as he had been at Brands Hatch the year before. In 1986 his drive shaft broke at the start and his race was effectively finished seconds after the green light. So he was fortunate indeed that the race was stopped due to a first corner

61

crash with the result that he was able to start, and win, in the spare Williams. At Silverstone this year his clutch disintegrated during the final Sunday half hour practice. If it had lasted intact until the race . . .!

The British Grand Prix has a magic and charisma all of its own. Since 1963 it has alternated between Silverstone and Brands Hatch but now, as a result of a contentious decision, it is due to be held at the Northamptonshire circuit for the next five years. A million pounds had been spent during the past year on improving Silverstone's facilities. New pits. New bridges. A much needed access tunnel. Two new corners in the place of the previous 'too fast' Woodcote Chicane. With superb weather for practicing the ex-World War Two airfield, thick with colourful hospitality tents and swollen with thousands of cars and excited, enthusiastic spectators had never looked better. And somehow, although it is always superbly organised and administered there is always a uniquely relaxed and carefree atmosphere at the British Grand Prix. It is difficult, for instance, to imagine this year's 'Fun Run' happening anywhere else. On Friday evening some 400 Centre Pass holders — the very core of the British GP — turned out to run the three mile Silverstone lap just for the sheer fun of it and to raise money for the Save the Children Fund. James Hunt ran. Eddie Cheever and Derek Warwick ran. Bernie Ecclestone pushed Frank Williams in his wheel chair. Clay Regazzoni propelled himself in his. Sir Jack Brabham walked! Martin Brundle confined himself to presenting the prizes. But a jolly good time was had by all and the Save the Children Fund immediately benefited by over £3,500 with some £7,000 more expected when the sponsorship promises were called in. A memorable event which will now, no doubt, become an annual fixture.

Silverstone, like most modern circuits, is flat. Its wide excellent surface embraces the old airfield perimeter road and its 2.96 mile lap is good for an average of nearly 160 mph — even with the new Woodcote corner and today's reduced-boost, race tyre restrictions. Precision driving, tyre conservation and fuel-efficiency are the name of the game and by the end of practice the Williams-Hondas had

shown, as in France, that if they kept going they were going to be very hard to beat.

Pole for Piquet. His first of the year. Second on the grid for Mansell after a spectacular effort to oust his team mate ended in clouds of dust at Woodcote following a late practice spin. Nevertheless, this was his seventh front row place in seven races and a mere 12/100 of a second slower than Nelson. Senna third in the Lotus, a full second slower, underlined the Honda engine's superiority but before the race even started it was clear that, as in France, the Lotus 'Active' suspension wasn't the benefit it had been on the street circuits and that with the Williams team's greater experience of Honda power they'd got a better all-round package than Lotus in terms of handling, aerodynamics, grip and fuel efficiency. Alain Prost, winner of the last two Silverstone British Grands Prix in 1983 (Renault) and 1985 (McLaren) was going for the hat trick but fourth on the grid, looked unlikely to achieve it in a McLaren that had given him a variety of practice problems and whose TAG engine was clearly not as effective as the Honda.

Behind the Top Three Constructors, Williams, McLaren and Lotus, came the Benettons and the Ferraris and neither of them was entirely happy. After their problems in France the superb-handling Benettons were running with reduced power from their Ford engines in an effort to achieve reliability despite which team-mates Boutsen and Fabi took fifth and sixth places on the grid — but over two seconds a lap slower than Piquet/Mansell. And that's a lot! The proud Ferrari team's bad patch continued. John Barnard, struggling to improve a car he hadn't designed, whilst simultaneously producing a new one for 1988, had had no time since the French debacle to effect improvements to the F187. Alboreto seventh and Berger eighth on the grid — and struggling. In the 3½ litre class it was Alliot's (Lola) turn to be fastest — twenty-first and nearly ten seconds slower than the Williams men. The normally aspirated cars were really suffering from their comparative lack of speed at Silverstone's power circuit.

But the one who was suffering most was the amiable Italian Piercarlo Ghinzani who, on Friday, was excluded from any further practising and the race, when he refuelled on the

De Cesaris almost on four wheels got really 'fired-up' later!

Team Analysis

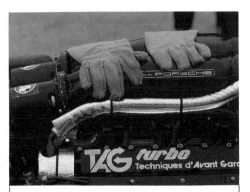

Prost likes them hot!

McLAREN

A demoralising race for the team which had won Silverstone's last two British Grands Prix. Prost qualifies fourth (top non-Honda engine). Races third until lap 30 tyre stop. Retires from fourth lap 54 (engine). No points. Down to fourth in Championship five points behind leader Senna. Johansson starts unimpressive tenth. Improves to sixth by lap eight. Retires lap nineteen (engine). Team retain second place Constructors Championship but now 21 points behind Williams. More reliable power needed to challenge Honda-engine teams.

TYRRELL

Two-days post-France wind tunnel testing in effort to improve straightline performance but, like all 3½ litre teams, severely affected by comparative lack of speed at horsepower circuit. Streiff/Palmer qualify 22/23. Race together up to excellent 8/9 on lap 54. Streiff retires lap 58 (engine). Palmer finishes eighth and wins class to extend Jim Clark Trophy lead.

WILLIAMS

Second successive crushing performance by team. Both cars on front row of grid. First and second in race to score maximum Constructors points and extend Championship lead over McLaren to 21 Points. Piquet takes first pole position of 1987 at nearly 160 mph. Leads race non-stop for virtually whole distance but, with failing grip, passed by Mansell on lap 63 of 65. Finishes second for fifth time in seven races. Retains Championship second place but now joined by Mansell. Mansell starts from front row (second) seventh time in seven races after post warm-up clutch change. Superbly overcomes 28 second deficit on Piquet to win third GP of year by 1.9 seconds after being forced to stop for tyres (lap 35) due to car imbalance caused by loss of wheel weight. Moves up to second equal (with Piquet) in Championship one point behind Senna.

BRABHAM

Disappointing race for team who give impression of lacking top level interest and direction. Patrese qualifies eleventh. Progresses to praiseworthy sixth by lap nineteen. Retires lap 29 (fuel meter/misfire). De Cesaris starts ninth in car rebuilt after French GP fire but retires after another conflagration at Becketts (lap eight).

ZAKSPEED

Straight to Silverstone after French GP for intensive wheel changing practice! After starting 17th Brundle delayed by two stops (tyres/throttle cable/EMS black box). Continues slowly to complete 54 laps (unclassified). Danner 18th on grid. Retires at back of field lap 33 (gearbox).

LOTUS

In spite of Honda power Lotus again inferior to Williams on fast circuit — attributable to comparative lack of experience with engine and development of total car/new motor 'package'. Senna third on grid and in race (lapped by Mansell and Piquet). Championship lead reduced to one point. Nakajima drives consistent race from twelfth on grid to finish fourth (two laps down). Third points finish in his first seven Grands Prix. Team Lotus retain third in Constructors Championship — now only two points behind McLaren.

Lotus boss Peter Warr watches Nakajima getting on TV.

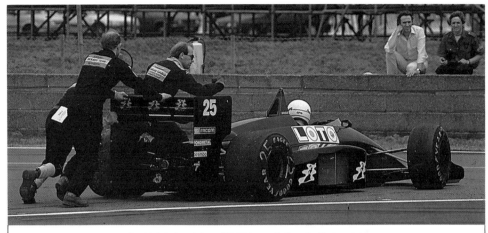

'I said right hand down!' British marshals make their point.

AGS

Fabre starts 25th and last. Another steady and slow but reliable race to ninth place six laps down. Their 100% finish record maintained with team and driver now both second in class championships.

MARCH

Capelli qualifies 24th and races to 18th on lap one but retires lap four with gearbox failure and engine fire.

ARROWS

Arrows now notably the 'Best of the Rest' — fifth in Constructors Championship. Derek Warwick at last finishes a race — in the points at fifth after starting 13th with new chassis. Cheever starts 14th, progresses to eighth (lap 29) but retires lap 46 (head gasket/overheating).

At last! Warwick cheers himself and his British fans with a fine fifth place.

BENETTON

Ford engines detuned for reliability after French GP problems. Nevertheless good grid positions for Boutsen (fifth) and Fabi (sixth) Fabi 'slowly' races to second successsive points finish (sixth — two laps down) with fuel consumption problem. Boutsen finishes seventh in spite of acute understeer, lost wheel balance weight, puncture and sticking throttle! Total chassis/engine package slowly improving. More reliable power needed.

OSELLA

Caffi qualifies 20th. Retires from twelfth place lap 33 (turbo fire).

MINARDI

Another depressing GP. Campos again demonstrates lack of experience by taking off Alliot at 160 mph during first practice. Starts 19th. Retires 12th (lap 33) with fuel pump malfunction. Nannini loses nosecone in start line incident (15th on grid). Fits new unit and rejoins last. Stays there until lap eleven retirement (engine).

LIGIER

Disastrous meeting for Guy Ligier's team. Ghinzani excluded from meeting after Friday first practice (refuelling on circuit and ignoring end-of-practice chequered flag.) Arnoux qualifies 16th but retires lap four (engine failure). Things must get better — they can't get worse!

FERRARI

Gloom after French debacle compounded by greater gloom after Britain. Team efficiency greatly inhibited by internal politics and lack of acceptable direction ('Barnard versus the rest' problem continues). Tragic situation for great team. Drivers complain of lack of power — unique problem for Ferrari. Alboreto seventh on grid. Races to fifth on lap three. Retires from lap 53 (rear suspension). Berger starts eighth, drops back to twelfth, improves to tenth only to spin into Abbey Curve armco and retirement (lap eight). Ferrari retain fourth in Constructors Championship a massive 43 points behind leaders (Williams).

LOLA

Alliot very lucky to escape uninjured when pushed off circuit by inexperienced Campos 160 mph during Friday first practice. Qualifies 21st (fastest 3½ litre car but nine seconds slower than Piquet pole time). Improves to 17th in race (lap five) but retires lap eight (transmission).

class lead. Andrea De Cesaris out with an even bigger fire than he'd had in France! Berger (Ferrari) out with a spin at the 175 mph Abbey Curve which ended in the Armco ('entirely my fault'). And, on lap twenty, poor Stefan Johansson's race finished with an engine failure after he'd climbed from tenth on the grid to sixth in only five laps.

It was on lap thirty, with Patrese having just retired from sixth place in favour of the hard-charging Nakajima, that what had seemed a static race came to life as Mansell reported his vibration problem via his car-to-pit radio and Prost changed his tyres — rejoining in fifth place behind Senna and Alboreto.

Lap 35. With a massive 35 second lead over the third man, Senna, Nigel Mansell detached his Williams nose from Piquet's gearbox and

The sky's the limit! Palmer in the purple panorama finished eighth and won his class. Nannini in the deadly nightshade failed to finish for the seventh time in seven races.

circuit (against the rules), was push-started by his mechanics (against the rules) and twice ignored the end-of-practice chequered flag (yes, of course it was!). So 25 to start the British Grand Prix.

Which turned out to be two races for the price of one. Piquet versus Mansell. And the rest fighting amongst themselves.

With a magnificent start Prost briefly led away only to succumb to the superior Honda power of first Piquet and Mansell on lap one and then Senna on lap two. But on lap five the World Champion re-took Senna and the third place he was to hold until his tyre stop. Piquet, Mansell, Prost, Senna and Alboreto held the first five places with some fifty seconds covering them by lap 29 but behind them there was a rapidly decaying field.

Arnoux out lap one (engine). Capelli too, from the lead of the 3½ litre class and eighteenth overall, with gearbox damage and an engine fire. Alliot out on lap eight with a broken transmission — to let the battling Tyrrells of Palmer and Streiff into the 3½ litre

Mansell 'in the finest race of his career' — quite brilliant.

hurtled into his pit for the unscheduled stop that was, paradoxically, to help win him the race. For, after the Goodyear technicians had examined both Prost and Mansell's first sets of tyres and pronounced that they would have gone the whole distance Piquet's pit crew gave him the signal 'Tyres OK, 22 laps' (to go). But they weren't as we all progressively saw. Lap 36. Mansell still second but now on new, grippier rubber. Lap 46. Nigel rockets round at a new lap record speed of nearly 151 mph. With eighteen laps to go Piquet's lead is down to eighteen seconds. Twelve laps left and it is 9.6 seconds. With the crowd roaring him to victory Mansell can do it! Lap 53. Mansell, gaining fast, laps at 152.9 mph. Lap 58 another record at a superb 153.1. And on that historic lap 63 he almost bangs wheels at Stowe as he passes Piquet on his way to victory. He

finishes with 'Minus 2½ laps' showing on his fuel counter. (Typically Williams had built a reserve into their calculations). Nigel had gambled everything and succeeded magnificently. He won his tenth Grand Prix with his third successive victory in Britain. He'd moved from fourth to second in the World Championship and, even more importantly from his point of view, he's made the Williams 1987 team wins score read 'Mansell 3: Piquet 0'.

But Silverstone was not, in any way, Prost's day. He never recovered from his pit stop, sadly retiring from fourth place on lap 54 (clutch and electrics) to be replaced by the steady and very quick Satoru Nakajima, once again finishing in the points at a circuit he now knew well. And with Senna third, although lapped as he had been a week earlier, Honda had achieved a crushing first four places.

Fabre's French 'tortoise' came home ninth. Alboreto's Italian 'hare' failed to finish.

The British Grand Prix was indeed a great day for Britain. A brilliant win for Mansell. First and second for the second time in succession for Williams. A popular and very well deserved first finish of the season for Derek Warwick (Arrows) in the points in the fifth place that Alboreto had held for so long before retiring. Eighth place overall and the class win for Jonathan Palmer's Tyrrell and British teams in the first eight places.

Honda-power was clearly and totally dominant — a fact which had to concern the other teams, especially McLaren, Ferrari and Arrows as they began their preparation for Germany.

BRITISH GRAND PRIX

Winner: Nigel Mansell, Williams FW11B/3   Fastest Lap: Nigel Mansell, 153.059 mph

GRID POSITION		RESULTS		
No.	Driver	Pos. Driver	Car	
6	Piquet	1 Mansell	Williams-Honda FW11B/3	
5	Mansell	2 Piquet	Williams-Honda FW11B/4	
12	Senna	3 Senna	Lotus-Honda 99T/4	
1	Prost	4 Nakajima	Lotus-Honda 99T/5	
20	Boutsen	5 Warwick	Arrows-Megatron A10/4	
19	Fabi	6 Fabi	Benetton-Ford B187-07	
27	Alboreto	7 Boutsen	Benetton-Ford B187-06	
28	Berger	8 Palmer	Tyrrell-Cosworth DG/016-2	
8	De Cesaris	9 Fabre	AGS-Cosworth JH22/02	
2	Johansson			
7	Patrese			
11	Nakajima			
17	Warwick			
18	Cheever			
24	Nannini			
25	Arnoux			
9	Brundle			
10	Danner			
23	Campos			
21	Caffi			
30	Alliot			
4	Streiff			
3	Palmer			
16	Capelli			
14	Fabre			

WORLD CHAMPIONSHIP				
Drivers		Pts	Constructors	Pts
1.	Senna	31	1. Williams-Honda	60
2.	Mansell	30	2. McLaren-TAG	39
	Piquet	30	3. Lotus-Honda	37
4.	Prost	26	4. Ferrari	17
5.	Johansson	13	5. Arrows-Megatron	6
6.	Berger	9	6. Benetton-Ford	5
7.	Alboreto	8	7. Brabham-BMW	4
8.	Nakajima	6	8. Tyrrell-Cosworth	3
9.	Cheever	4	9. Zakspeed	2
	De Cesaris	4	10. Ligier-Megatron	1
11.	Fabi	3	March-Cosworth	1
12.	Boutsen	2		
	Brundle	2		
	Palmer	2		
	Warwick	2		
16.	Arnoux	1		
	Capelli	1		
	Streiff	1		

JIM CLARK CUP			COLIN CHAPMAN CUP		
1.	Palmer	42	1. Tyrrell-Cosworth		72
2.	Fabre	32	2. AGS-Cosworth		32
3.	Streiff	30	3. Lola-Cosworth		15
4.	Alliot	15	4. March-Cosworth		6
5.	Capelli	6			

GERMANY

26th July 1987
Circuit: Hockenheim

'THERE'S a positive side to it,' said Ron Dennis, the McLaren boss, 'we're fully back in contention again.' Indeed they were. In the last two Grands Prix neither Prost nor Johansson had scored a single point and the mighty McLaren team were looking distinctly groggy with an engine vibration problem that had worried them a lot more than they were prepared to admit in public.

With their home Grand Prix at Hockenheim, Porsche, who designed and build McLaren's TAG engines, made a maximum effort to get things right, finding in the process that the crankshafts were improperly balanced. A major problem for whoever was supposed to have done the job but one easily overcome. Three revised engines were delivered to the team and in both practice and the race it was very clear that they were right back with Williams. Nothing stays the same in Formula One for long!

The Hockenheim-Ring, near the beautiful University city of Heidelberg, is flat, very fast (1986 lap record 142.6 mph; Gerhard Berger/ Benetton BMW) and mostly very dull. It has a long lap — 4.2 miles — and most of it comprises two shallow, flat out curves which, seemingly endlessly, bore through solid vertical cliffs of gloomy pine forest. Each curve has an artificial chicane to slow things down from over 210 mph to about 95 mph and they're connected at the top by a sweeping, once

Grand Prix racing would be nowhere without Goodyear.

spectacular, bend which was also given a chicane after the tragic 1980 death there, in testing, of Frenchman Patrick Depailler. Joining the curves at the bottom is the twisty bit that's mostly seen on TV — the impressive Stadium section. Impressive because the short five bend segment is literally surrounded by gigantic, towering concrete grandstands which can hold some 100,000 spectators. That's where most of the action takes place and if the crowd likes what it sees the drivers tell me they can hear the roar of approval over their engines! It's the nearest Grand Prix equivalent there is to the gladiatorial amphitheatres of Ancient Rome.

To Hockenheim then they came, for the halfway point of the 1987 World Championship — Round eight. Knowing it is a circuit that is notoriously hard on engines. Knowing that it is very difficult indeed to set up a car to get the best compromise between straight line speed and handling necessitated by the long fast curves, the chicanes and the sinuous Stadium. And knowing that, most of all, getting the fuel consumption right is absolutely critical. Keke Rosberg and Alain Prost, second and fourth in their McLarens, both ran out on the last lap in 1986!

As if the race engineers and drivers hadn't got enough problems the weather compound-

69

'No wonder I am only 24th on the grid — I've been turning left instead of right!' Capelli swats up on Hockenheim geography.

ed them. With practising, as usual, on Friday and Saturday the normal expectation applied — that the starting grid positions would be finalised in the closing minutes of Saturday's sixty minute qualifying session after lunch. But not this time! To say that it rained would be a masterpiece of understatement. Water hosepiped down from low black clouds you felt you could poke a finger through and only fifteen of the twenty-six entrants turned a wheel — in mortal fear of aquaplaning. Ever mindful, too, of the hideous crash that had shattered the late Didier Pironi's legs in 1982 when, flat out he hurtled his Ferrari into an impenetrable ball of grey spray that contained Alain Prost's Renault.

So it was Friday's times that decided the starting grid. A confident, cheerful Nigel Mansell in pole position for the sixth time in the year's eight races — only six-tenths of a second slower than Keke Rosberg's 1986 time. And for the fourth time it was Ayrton Senna alongside him, happy with his 'Active' Lotus-Honda and a mere one-fifth second slower than the Williams. Third was Prost delighted with the speed, the handling and the fuel consumption of his re-engined McLaren and optimistic about taking his score of Grand Prix wins to a record 28. Piquet was a gloomy fourth after a Friday when both car and engine had given him problems and a wet Saturday when he couldn't improve his time. The Ferraris had had a mixed time — Alboreto fifth but Berger only tenth after having his special rear wing stolen by a souvenir hunter when he'd crashed on Friday! The Benettons were in good shape; Boutsen sixth and Fabi ninth with revised Ford Turbomotors giving more power and better fuel consumption. But at Hockenheim, to no-one's surprise, the 3½ litre cars were ten seconds off the pace with Alliot's Lola highest at 21st. 'They'll be mobile chicanes here,' we thought. But how wrong we were!

Sunday, thank heavens, was a dry day. No one wants to race at Hockenheim when it's wet. Not even 'Rain King' Eddie Cheever. With a magnificent start Senna took the lead in his spare Lotus, having been unhappy with his race car's handling in the morning's half hour warm-up in spite of his satisfaction the day before. Followed by Prost! The Frenchman wound up the McLaren and surged past Mansell before the long drag through the forest only to be passed by the Williams-Honda halfway round the lap. Into the Stadium it was Senna, Mansell, Prost, Piquet, Boutsen, Alboreto and Johansson — the start of a seven car battle that was to enthral Hockenheim's thousands and TV's millions for lap after lap. With the Lotus soon down to fourth as Senna grappled with acute understeer, two seconds covered Mansell, Prost, Piquet and Senna. Close behind, Boutsen's Benetton nosecone was practically sawing Alboreto's gearbox in two as the Belgian jinked from side to side in his efforts to pass the Ferrari.

Lap eight. Sensation! Prost neatly, smoothly

Streiff's practice shunt did not stop him scoring a brilliant fourth place.

From seventh to oblivion — a frustrated Derek Warwick leaves his turbo fire.

Team Analysis

McLAREN

Back in contention! Engine vibration problem in last two races found to be due to crankshaft imbalance. Revised TAG units supplied by Porsche for major effort in their home GP. Prost signs for two more years with team and qualifies happy and confident third (fastest in Sunday warm up). Races brilliantly to lead on lap eight. Holds it commandingly for 28 laps but retires lap 40 with broken alternator belt. No points. Still fourth Drivers Championship thirteen points behind new leader Piquet. Johansson qualifies eighth. Races to sixth lap ten. Improves to third lap 26 through retirements. Finishes excellent second with totally shredded front right tyre and collapsed suspension. Still fifth in Championship. Team retain Constructors Championship second place but now 24 points behind Williams.

TYRRELL

Team's best 1987 race to date. Totally against expectations both cars finish in top six only one lap behind winner. Just-married Palmer qualifies 23rd and races whole distance with team mate Streiff. Finishes superb fifth. Retains Jim Clark trophy lead. Streiff, 22nd on grid, out-qualifies Palmer and just beats him in race to finish magnificent fourth (best 3½ litre place so far). Now second in Jim Clark Trophy contest and eleventh in Drivers Championship. Team Tyrrell up to fifth in Constructors Championship — ahead of seven turbo teams.

WILLIAMS

A sweet and sour race for Team Williams. Mansell takes sixth pole position from eight races. Fastest in both Friday dry and Saturday wet practices. Leads for eight laps but retires from strong and challenging second on lap 26 with dead engine. Piquet qualifies fourth after unhappy practice (car and engine problems Friday: unable to improve on wet Saturday). Races third hampered by lack of information from blank instruments VDU. Benefits from Mansell (lap 26) and Prost (lap 40) retirements and return of VDU to win first GP of season and take World Championship lead at halfway stage. Team increases Constructors Championship lead over McLaren to impressive 24 points.

BRABHAM

Twenty-fifth anniversary of first-ever Brabham GP car appearance at Nurburgring. Further work on aerodynamics and BMW engine. Very disheartening race. Patrese qualifies eleventh with new monocoque. Retires from last position lap six (electrics). De Cesaris starts seventh. Retires from same position lap 13 (major engine blow-up).

ZAKSPEED

Important but heart-breaking home race for the Niederzissen team — cheekily carrying 'EAST' logos to thumb noses at German law forbidding display of 'WEST' cigarette sponsorship! Brundle car with major suspension, aerodynamic,

The Hockenheim Stadium — a motor-racing amphitheatre.

Honda engine seize? Mansell's did. It spoiled a great scrap with Prost.

engine and transmission changes qualifies 19th after disastrous practice. Immediate electronics problem in race. Frequent pit stops. Martin runs last to complete 34 laps. Unclassified and disheartened. Danner even worse. Qualifies 20th. Retires lap 12 when thirteenth (electrics and broken drive shaft). Sad day for gallant team.

LOTUS

Team Manager Peter Warr describes Team Lotus as being '2% behind Williams' in terms of aerodynamic and fuel efficiency. Major revisions being finalised for next GP (Hungary). Nevertheless Senna qualifies second for 'fourth front row with Mansell' grid position of season. Starts race in spare Lotus after warm-up dissatisfaction with race car. Leads lap one. Has three pit stops (tyre change/Active suspension check/replacement nose aerofoils). Finishes excellent third (considering that his boost control had failed and that his 'Active' suspension oil reservoir had leaked dry). Drops to second in Championship four points behind Piquet. Nakajima suffers 'Active' suspension problems in practice and race. Qualifies fourteenth. Retires lap nine when thirteenth. Team Lotus retain third in Constructors Championship.

AGS

Fabre qualifies 25th in unchanged car and retires for first time in eight races due to over-revving on lap ten when twentieth.

MARCH

Revised fuel system since Silverstone. First time at Hockenheim for ebullient Capelli. ('Easy to learn: hard to master!') Qualifies 24th. Starts race from pit lane after spark box problems with race car. Retires from 23rd, lap eight, with common Ford DFZ problem — broken rotor arm.

ARROWS

New, low downforce, rear wing. Improved fuel consumption from Heini Mader-developed Megatron engine. Warwick improves from 13th on grid to seventh by lap 20 but retires with massive turbo fire, lap 24. Cheever races with Warwick from 15th on grid but retires from twelfth, lap ten, with broken throttle linkage. Arrows no longer 'Best of the Rest' — down to sixth in Constructors Championship behind normally-aspirated Tyrrells.

BENETTON

'Still learning about the car' says Designer Rory Byrne. Three different specifications of Ford Turbo engine for Hockenheim — more power and better fuel efficiency. But not good

enough. Boutsen and Fabi qualify sixth and ninth. Both eliminated by major engine failures — Fabi when seventh (lap 17) and Boutsen (lap 27) having raced excellent fourth behind Prost, Mansell and Piquet. Team slide to disappointing seventh in Constructors Championship.

OSELLA

Alex Caffi starts 26th and last. Races to 21st lap four. Drops to last and retires lap 18 (engine).

MINARDI

A promising race destroyed by usual inadequate Motori Moderni engine. Nannini and Campos qualify sixteenth and eighteenth and race to seventh and ninth out of thirteen runners then left (lap 24). Nannini engine seizes lap 26. Campos out lap 29 (engine).

LIGIER

Appalling meeting for the respected Vichy team still beset with major Megatron engine and/or installation problems. Four motors destroyed by Arnoux and Ghinzani in practice (at some £40,000 each!) Arnoux twelfth on grid. Electronic problems from lap three. Retires from last place lap seven. Almost Ghinzani's best race ever. Advances to fifth (out of nine left) but despondently retires (again) lap 32. With no time for essential development between Grands Prix difficult to see how Ligier can get out of morass.

The chicane slows things down just a little — here Patrese leading Capelli.

FERRARI

Exactly two years since last Ferrari win (Nurburgring 1985: Alboreto). Yet more John Barnard-inspired revisions to inadequate Gustav Brunner design. Aerodynamic, suspension, air-intake and engine changes. Major problem continues to be comparative lack of power. Alboreto happy to qualify fifth (third fastest Sunday warm-up). Races strongly in fifth place but retires lap eleven (left-side turbo). After crashing in Friday timed practice Berger has 'one-off' development rear wing stolen by souvenir hunter! Eventually qualifies tenth. Retires from struggling sixth (lap 20) — also with left-side turbo failure. Legendary Maranello team now scored only seventeen points in eight 1987 races.

LOLA

Good race for Gerard Larrousse's efficient and popular team. Alliot again qualifies as fastest 3½ litre (21st). Finishes excellent sixth even though hampered by engine management system fault which limits revs to 9,000.

Stefan on three wheels earns superb six points. If he'd only had the full set . . .

and effortlessly sliced past Mansell's Williams to lead the German Grand Prix until his lap nineteen tyre stop. Lap ten and the hapless Alboreto fell back to retire for the fifth time in eight races (this time with a broken turbo) and let the forceful Boutsen into fifth place. And Johansson to sixth.

Meantime Piquet in third position was dropping back from the enthralling Prost/Mansell battle for the lead. Something had to be wrong. It was! Nelson was driving 'blind' with no information from a blank instruments visual display unit. No knowledge of his fuel consumption — and that's bad news at Hockenheim. 'Frank Dernie (race engineer) was giving me information over the radio but it's not the same.' So all the winner of the 1986 German Grand Prix (and 1981) could do was soldier on as fast as he dared and hope that the leaders would strike trouble.

Lap 26. On new tyres and with a record lap just completed at 144.65 mph Nigel Mansell had closed the gap between himself and leader Prost to 3.5 seconds — and was gaining. When his engine seized. That's racing. No recriminations. Out of the car, over the Armco, into the Learjet and back home to

the Isle of Man. In time to watch the BBC TV highlights of the race that could have given him back the lead in the World Championship.

So now Piquet was second — 'but no way could I have caught Alain even though my VDU had come alive to show me I was OK for fuel. So I turned up the boost and was catching him by two seconds a lap. But it was too late.'

It wasn't! Fate at last smiled on Nelson. Five laps from the chequered flag and seemingly on his way to his sixth second place from six 1987 finishes he saw the distinctive red and white McLaren on the grass with a dispirited Prost clambering out.

Minutes later Nelson Piquet won his first Grand Prix of the year, and the eighteenth of his career, to take the lead in the World Championship — a victory which may have been his by default but which was richly deserved. Prost? After he'd ridden back to the pits on the sidepod of Piquet's Williams he said one word, 'Alternator.' A broken belt had robbed him of that record 28th win just as it had robbed him of second place at Imola and

Johansson of sixth place in France. But Stefan had his consolation in Germany with one of the most spectacular finishes we'd seen for years — second place driving on the brake disc as his right front tyre punctured approaching the Stadium on the last lap!

With Senna third and lapped for the third GP in succession, hardly surprising at Hockenheim for in the closing stages of the race his 'Active' suspension's hydraulic oil had disappeared leaving him to finish on the metal slave springs, and with only seven classified finishers from the 26 who'd started, a totally unexpected highlight of the German Grand Prix was that the fourth, fifth and sixth places were taken by the 'outclassed' 3½ litre cars of Streiff and Palmer (Tyrrells) and Philippe Alliot's Lola. What is more the Tyrrells were on the same lap as Senna, only one lap behind Piquet, and less than a second from each other after a thrilling race-long battle.

So history had repeated itself. Mansell won in Britain and France in 1986 and '87 followed, both years, by Piquet victories in Germany. The next Grand Prix was to be Hungary's second. And Piquet had won there in 1986 . . .

Piquet — fast, smooth and lucky.

Not renowned for carrying passengers, Piquet gives lift to disappointed Prost.

GERMAN GRAND PRIX

Winner: Nelson Piquet, Williams FW11B/4   *Fastest Lap:* Nigel Mansell, 143.854 mph

GRID POSITION		RESULTS			WORLD CHAMPIONSHIP			
No.	*Driver*	*Pos.*	*Driver*	*Car*	*Drivers*	*Pts*	*Constructors*	*Pts*
5	Mansell	1	Piquet	Williams-Honda FW11B/4	1. Piquet	39	1. Williams-Honda	69
12	Senna	2	Johansson	McLaren-TAG MP4/3C-2	2. Senna	35	2. McLaren-TAG	45
1	Prost	3	Senna	Lotus-Honda 99T/4	3. Mansell	30	3. Lotus-Honda	41
6	Piquet	4	Streiff	Tyrrell-Cosworth DG/016-3	4. Prost	26	4. Ferrari	17
27	Alboreto	5	Palmer	Tyrrell-Cosworth DG/016-2	5. Johansson	19	5. Tyrrell-Cosworth	8
20	Boutsen	6	Alliot	Lola-Cosworth LC87/03	6. Berger	9	6. Arrows-Megatron	6
8	De Cesaris	7	Prost	McLaren-TAG MP4/3C-3	7. Alboreto	8	7. Benetton-Ford	5
2	Johansson	8	Brundle	Zakspeed 871/3	8. Nakajima	6	8. Brabham-BMW	4
19	Fabi				9. Cheever	4	9. Zakspeed	2
28	Berger				De Cesaris	4	10. Ligier-Megatron	1
7	Patrese				Palmer	4	Lola-Cosworth	1
25	Arnoux				Streiff	4	March-Cosworth	1
17	Warwick				13. Fabi	3		
11	Nakajima				14. Boutsen	2		
18	Cheever				Brundle	2		
24	Nannini				Warwick	2		
26	Ghinzani				17. Alliot	1		
23	Campos				Arnoux	1		
9	Brundle				Capelli	1		
10	Danner							
30	Alliot				**JIM CLARK CUP**		**COLIN CHAPMAN CUP**	
4	Streiff				1. Palmer	48	1. Tyrrell-Cosworth	87
3	Palmer				2. Streiff	39	2. AGS-Cosworth	32
16	Capelli				3. Fabre	32	3. Lola-Cosworth	19
14	Fabre				4. Alliot	19	4. March-Cosworth	6
21	Caffi				5. Capelli	6		

HUNGARY

9th August 1987
Circuit: Hungaroring

THIS was to be Hungary's second World Championship race and the whole Grand Prix scene returned to the land of the Magyars with enormous enthusiasm with one of four men seemingly certain to take the top honour — Piquet, Senna, Mansell or Prost. In 1986 when we first went there it was with some concern and an edgy feeling of insecurity. What was it going to be like behind the Iron Curtain? Would they be able to cope with the sophisticated demands of Formula One? Would it all be grey and miserable? We needn't have worried!

The Hungarians were delightful. Friendly, kind, helpful and cheerful. The specially built 2.5 mile Hungaroring turned out to be an absolutely magnificent venue which lacked nothing. The organisers and officials had visited other Grands Prix, asked for advice, taken it and acted on it. The Ring's location is perfect. Twelve miles or so from the truly beautiful and impressive city of Budapest on the River Danube, with its cosmopolitan atmosphere and stunning architecture, it straddles a deep valley which provides the gradient that so many Grand Prix circuits lack.

The hillsides provide perfect natural vantage points for the colossal crowds (200,000 in 1986!) and the lap comprises an excellent blend of fast and slow, uphill and downhill, corners with a flat out straight past the enormous grandstand and excellent pits. The organisation was immaculate and the facilities were five star. In short Hungary was good! Everybody liked the circuit, the people, the city of Budapest and the fact that, with motorway travel from the city hotels to the circuit, access was fast and easy. And just to add the final touch the weather was superb!

That was 1986. 1987 was even better. With grass where, the year before, there had been bare earth, with the facilities added-to and improved beyond even their previous high standards there was a feeling of well-being and a vibrant atmosphere in the paddock on the first morning of practice. But the buzz of excitement was nothing to do with the Hungaroring! It was caused by an announce-

Despondently not 'Vorsprung Durch Technik'. Martin Brundle's Zakspeed goes West again.

ment that electrified the Grand Prix scene — Ayrton Senna was leaving the Lotus team at the end of the season to be replaced by Nelson Piquet!

As any season wears on there are always rumours about who is going where next year but this was hard fact and an unusually early move. For reasons we could only guess Senna had implemented his right to terminate his Lotus contract at the end of the year. With lightning rapidity Team Manager Peter Warr had contacted Nelson Piquet who had, for some time, been openly critical of what he believed to be the failure of the Williams' team to give him the 'Number One Driver' treatment which his contract stipulated. In five days the deal was done. Piquet for Lotus in 1988!

So the already highly-charged atmosphere in Hungary became supercharged with un-answered questions and speculative gossip. What was Senna up to? Where was he going? Had he signed with McLaren already? Were Williams going to lose their Honda engines in 1988? Were McLaren going to get them instead? Who would be the Williams' Number Two driver next year? Were Michelin coming

back into Formula One? The silly season had started early!

But at ten o'clock on Friday, 7th August the action took precedence with the first of the usual four practice periods in dull, cloudy and chilly weather. In the one-hour afternoon qualifying session the track was drying after rain and in the closing stages Nigel Mansell once again proved himself to be the class of the field with a searing lap in 1 minute 28.047 seconds (102.6 mph) — nearly 1½ seconds faster than Senna's 1986 pole position time in the super-boosted Lotus-Renault. Although Saturday's qualifying session was held in drier and warmer conditions only eleven out of the 26 entrants bettered their Friday times and none of them beat Nigel's. So for the seventh time in nine meetings Mansell was to start in pole position — a richly deserved 33rd birth-day present to himself!

In second place on the grid was something we hadn't seen since Germany in 1985 — a Ferrari! Engineering Director John Barnard had declared his intention to stay away from the next five Grands Prix (including Italy?) 'to finish designing a Ferrari that will win in 1988'. But under his control the steady development

Ferrari seemed to be improving — Berger second on grid. Alboreto fifth. But neither finished.

Another six points — Senna's reliable Lotus-Honda keeps him second in championship.

of the glorious looking scarlet 187 was getting there too. Sick with flu and stomach cramps he may have been but Gerhard Berger was second fastest with Michele Alboreto fifth behind Piquet (third) and Prost but ahead of Senna who had been severely troubled — as had the rest of them — by a distinct lack of grip at the Hungaroring.

It was going to be a long hard race. Every team planned to go the 190 miles with no tyre changes and it would take almost the maximum permissible two hours to cover the scheduled 76 laps. Hardly an enthralling prospect for Berger, Piquet and Warwick, all of whom were suffering from the after-effects of a local stomach and flu virus.

In the words of Nigel Mansell 'pole position here is every bit as important as it is at Monaco because of the passing problem. There's a big advantage for the man in front at the off.' To prove it he departed like a shot from a gun to

take the lead with a perfect start. A lead he brilliantly held for 70 laps. 70 laps? In a 76 lap race? Precisely! Nigel Mansell's sickening German experience was to be repeated and the 86/87 pattern of victories was to be continued in Hungary.

In the opening laps as Mansell smoothly and impressively raced to a seemingly inevitable fourth win of the season, there was a magnificent sight behind him. The Ferraris of Berger and Alboreto in second and third places and, at times, right up with the leader in his Williams-Honda. The Prancing Horse was back and didn't the crowd love it!

For twelve laps they were sandwiched between Mansell and Piquet with Senna and Boutsen (Benetton) nose-to-tail in fifth and sixth places ahead of the McLarens of Johansson and Prost — both of which had power-sapping intermittent misfires.

Lap 13: a groan from the vast crowd as

79

Team Analysis

McLAREN

Disappointing race after improved form in Germany. McLaren, as all teams, find it difficult to get grip on smooth track surface. Prost qualifies satisfactory fourth but hampered by persistent misfire in race. Finishes distant third to move to third equal (with Mansell) in championship. Johansson starts eighth. Passes Prost and improves to sixth lap 14 in spite of misfire. Retires next lap after spin (just missing Prost!) caused by broken crown wheel. Remains fifth but, with only 19 points, out of contention in Championship. Team still second in Constructors Championship but 29 points behind Williams and only two ahead of Lotus.

TYRRELL

Aerodynamic changes for 'slow' Hungaroring — notably new undertray. New chassis for Palmer who starts 16th on grid. Catches and passes team mate Streiff to finish excellent seventh, two laps down, and win class for fifth time. Extends lead in 3½ litre championship. Streiff starts 14th as fastest in class (5½ seconds off the pace) and similarly has good race — except for broken exhaust pipe. Team now unbeatable in 'Atmospheric' Constructors Championship.

Another lucky win for Piquet — this time at Mansell's expense.

WILLIAMS

Celebrating 33rd birthday at Hungaroring Mansell again superbly dominates practice to achieve seventh pole position in nine races — some 1½ seconds faster than Senna 1986 time. Brilliantly controls race from front until lap 71 out of 76 when forced to retire as wheel nut departs hub. This cruelly robbed of certain victory for second successive race. Piquet dramatically announces decision to join Lotus in 1988. Suffers from 'local' virus in practice but qualifies third. After catching and passing Berger and Alboreto Ferraris races behind Mansell seemingly to sixth second place of year. Unexpectedly inherits lead with Mansell retirement to win second successive GP (with record lap) suffering from severe tyre-induced vibration. Increases Championship lead to seven points over Senna and dominant eighteen over unfortunate Mansell. Team now lead McLaren in Constructors Championship by massive 29 points.

Alex Caffi trying to keep up the spirits of the hard-trying Osella team.

BRABHAM

Amidst rumours of Brabham sale to Athletico Madrid, Team Co-ordinator Colin Seeley joins exodus from unsettled team. Minor aerodynamic changes to suit twisty Hungaroring. Patrese starts tenth and races steadily to fifth, one lap down, to score his first points of season. De Cesaris improves to tenth from start 13th. Changes flat-spotted tyres after spin but retires lap 44 with broken gearbox.

ZAKSPEED

From bad in Germany to terrible in Hungary. 'We have gone wrong somewhere mechanically. Engine OK. Aerodynamics OK. But mechanically . . .!' Brundle starts 22nd after major electrical problems in Saturday and Sunday practice. Retires lap 45 with turbo failure when 13th. After starting 23rd Danner stops and retires with electrical defect lap four. Gloom and despondency abound.

LOTUS

Following Senna request for release from Lotus contract at season's end, fast moving Team Manager Peter Warr proudly announces Nelson Piquet appointed as replacement. Consternation all round. Senna future intentions not known. Reduced frontal area for both cars with revised engine cover, cockpit surround and side pods. First time for Nakajima at Hungaroring. Qualifies 17th. Breaks CV joint at start. Limps round one lap to retirement. Senna, much troubled by 'no grip' as result of combined effects of 'Active' suspension and smooth surface, qualifies lowly sixth (for him). Benefits from Berger, Alboreto and Mansell retirements to finish gritty second with acute back pain caused by major vibration as result of lost right front wheel weight and rear tyre moving round rim. Still second in Drivers Championship. Team Lotus now only two points behind second placed McLaren in Constructors Championship.

AGS

Fabre qualifies 26th and last. Finishes last again in thirteenth place out of 26 starters — but finishes! (Six laps down.) Fabre now third in Class Drivers Championship. AGS second in Constructors contest 67 points behind unbeatable two-car Tyrrell team.

MARCH

Joined by gifted designer Adrian Newey team efforts to improve reliability generate success. Capelli starts 18th and finishes 10th, only two laps down, with blistered left front tyre. Following dissatisfaction with Cosworth engines decision made to switch to 3½ litre 'Atmospheric' Honda power after Austrian GP.

ARROWS

Engine installation improvements, new brake ducts and new rear wing after German GP. Warwick in very poor shape with flu and conjunctivitis but nevertheless qualifies ninth. Hangs on to finish in points for second time in Arrows in worthy sixth place. Lifted from car in state of exhaustion. First time at Hungaroring for Cheever. Starts ninth. Finishes eighth despite puncturing Warwick rear tyre by driving into it and removing own nose wing! Team drop place to seventh in Constructors Championship.

BENETTON

Further work to improve reliability. After multitude of practice problems, Fabi starts twelfth. Retires lap 15 (gearbox). Boutsen qualifies seventh. Races sixth behind Senna unable to pass due to brake problems. Finishes fourth (lapped) with failing boost pressure. Boutsen's three points improve team position two places to fifth equal (with Tyrrell) in Constructors Championship.

OSELLA

Caffi qualifies 21st and lasts much longer than usual before retiring, lap 65, from 15th and last position with electrical and fuel pump problems.

MINARDI

Campos starts 24th. Ends lap 15 with spin into armco which removes rear wing and Campos from race. Nannini achieves first Minardi team finish in nine races in eleventh place, three laps down. Cause for celebration and encouragement for team to try harder for elusive reliability.

LIGIER

Bigger intercoolers and rear brake shrouds but little apparent improvement. Arnoux starts 19th and races with team mate Ghinzani before retiring from 14th on lap 57. Ghinzani achieves his third Ligier finish in twelfth place (three laps down) with a faltering Megatron engine after starting 25th.

Ghinzani actually finished in Hungary. But he finished twelfth.

FERRARI

Engineering Director John Barnard conspicuous by absence after announcing decision to miss next five GPs to finish designing new Ferrari. Nevertheless continued development of '87 car pleases drivers Alboreto and Berger. Berger, with flu and upset stomach, puts Ferrari on front row of grid (second) for first time since Germany, 1985. Alboreto qualifies fifth. Stirring sight as Berger/Alboreto race second and third until lap 13. Berger out (CV joint). Alboreto holds second until lap 28. Retires from third lap 44 (engine). Berger sixth and Alboreto seventh in Drivers Championship but completely out of touch. Team still fourth in Constructors contest but 61 points behind leaders, Williams after fourth successive 'no points' race.

LOLA

Alliot qualifies 15th. Retires lap 49 when 13th (lap two spin flat spots tyre. Resultant vibration cracks suspension wishbone which eventually breaks to cause further spin out of contention). Alliot fourth and team third in respective 3½ litre championships.

Benetton and Zakspeed side by side at Hungaroring.

Berger rolled to a standstill in front of the pits with a broken CV joint. So Alboreto to an impressive second followed by a slowly-gaining Nelson Piquet and, at an ever increasing distance, the continuing Senna/Boutsen duel (now for fourth) and Prost. Prost? Yes, for Stefan Johansson, having passed his faltering World Champion team mate's McLaren had spun out of contention as his crown wheel broke on lap 15 — nearly ramming Alain as he did so!

On lap 29 Piquet finally got past Alboreto to second place but, on lap 43, another huge collective groan signified the fact that Michele's Ferrari was out with a broken engine to let Patrese's Brabham move up to sixth. Yet another 'no points' race for Maranello — their fourth in a row. But try as he may Nelson could make no real impression on Mansell's lead. For every fastest lap — and then record lap — he made in an effort to close the ten second gap, Nigel cooly responded. So the Williams' team were going to score another magnificent first and second —

Great circuit. Great crowd. Great race.

with Senna third and the 'always there' Prost now up to fourth as Boutsen fell back a place with brake and boost problems.

It was not to be. For the second race in succession with only six laps to go and victory practically in sight, Mansell was out. TV viewers will long remember the sad sight of his Williams weaving from side to side as Nigel appeared to be running out of fuel. But the sharper-eyed saw a wheel nut fly off and bounce across the road to render his car undriveable. How could it have happened? 'A

mystery' said both Designer Patrick Head and Chief Mechanic Alan Challis. 'We torqued the wheel nuts up properly on the grid. There was no tyre stop. It shouldn't have happened.' But it did. Another lost victory for the blameless and utterly dejected Mansell.

So Nelson Piquet won, as he had in 1986. To extend his Championship lead and make Mansell's hopes of success look very dim. With Riccardo Patrese taking his first points of the season in fifth place behind Piquet, Senna, Prost and Boutsen a cheerful note was struck

In spite of this practice spin, Nigel took his seventh pole in nine meetings.

for Britain by Derek Warwick finishing sixth (and having to be lifted from the cockpit in a state of exhaustion) and Jonathan Palmer coming home on the same lap in seventh place to win the 3½ litre class for the fifth time and thus increase his lead in the 'Atmospheric' World Championship.

Williams now led the Constructors Championship by a massive 29 points and it was clear that unless McLaren and Lotus could do something very quickly to close the perform-

ance gap they would have to resign themselves to failure in 1987. It was equally clear that, with two wins and five second places now counting towards his best eleven results from the sixteen Championship races Nelson Piquet looked increasingly likely to be joining Lotus as World Champion in 1988.

A significant day in Hungary then. A day which was capped by Lotus Team Manager Peter Warr's saucy comment — 'I think both our chaps did rather well, don't you?'

AGS and Fabre are real triers — but they need a quicker car.

HUNGARIAN GRAND PRIX

Winner: Nelson Piquet, Williams FW11B/4   *Fastest Lap:* Nelson Piquet, 99.60 mph

GRID POSITION		RESULTS			WORLD CHAMPIONSHIP				
No.	Driver	Pos.	Driver	Car	Drivers	Pts	Constructors		Pts
5	Mansell	1	Piquet	Williams-Honda FW11B/4	1. Piquet	48	1. Williams-Honda		78
28	Berger	2	Senna	Lotus-Honda 99T/5	2. Senna	41	2. McLaren-TAG		49
6	Piquet	3	Prost	McLaren-TAG MP4/3C-3	3. Mansell	30	3. Lotus-Honda		47
1	Prost	4	Boutsen	Benetton-Ford B187-06	Prost	30	4. Ferrari		17
27	Alboreto	5	Patrese	Brabham-BMW BT56/4	5. Johansson	19	5. Benetton-Ford		8
12	Senna	6	Warwick	Arrows-Megatron A10/4	6. Berger	9	6. Tyrrell-Cosworth		8
20	Boutsen	7	Palmer	Tyrrell-Cosworth DG016-6	7. Alboreto	8	7. Brabham-BMW		6
2	Johansson	8	Cheever	Arrows-Megatron A10/3	8. Nakajima	6	8. Zakspeed		2
17	Warwick	9	Streiff	Tyrrell-Cosworth DG016-5	9. Boutsen	5	9. Ligier-Megatron		1
7	Patrese	10	Capelli	March-Cosworth 871/02	10. Cheever	4	Lola-Cosworth		1
18	Cheever	11	Nannini	Minardi-Moderni M186-03	De Cesaris	4	March-Cosworth		1
19	Fabi	12	Ghinzani	Ligier-Megatron JS29C-4	Palmer	4			
8	De Cesaris	13	Fabre	AGS-Cosworth JH22/02	Streiff	4			
4	Streiff				14. Fabi	3			
30	Alliot				Warwick	3			
3	Palmer				16. Brundle	2			
11	Nakajima				Patrese	2			
16	Capelli				18. Alliot	1			
25	Arnoux				Arnoux	1			
24	Nannini				Capelli	1			
21	Caffi								
9	Brundle				JIM CLARK CUP		COLIN CHAPMAN CUP		
10	Danner				1. Palmer	57	1. Tyrrell-Cosworth		102
23	Campos				2. Streiff	45	2. AGS-Cosworth		35
26	Ghinzani				3. Fabre	35	3. Lola-Cosworth		19
14	Fabre				4. Alliot	19	4. March-Cosworth		10
					5. Capelli	10			

AUSTRIA

16th August 1987
Circuit: Osterreichring

FROM the Hungaroring to the Osterreichring it is less than 250 miles. But they might as
well be on different planets — the 'Communist' Hungaroring is ultra-modern, highly
organised, slippery-smooth and twisty with a lap record of just under 100 miles an hour.
The 'Democratic' Osterreichring, at an altitude of 2,000 feet and set in a beautiful Styrian
valley surrounded by mountains has a quaintly 'established' — almost old-fashioned —
atmosphere, is notoriously bumpy and now has a lap record of just over 150 miles an hour.

But despite its deficiencies, which were to become frighteningly apparent, it is a circuit
the drivers both like and respect. No first gear corners here. No brake testing,
boost-inhibiting slow sections to delay the action and prove nothing. The Osterreichring is
a series of dauntingly fast straights and sweepers which separate the men from the
supermen and which generate a flat-out speed of over 215 miles an hour. The
never-ending, 160 miles an hour, right-handed Bosch Curve is one of Grand Prix racing's
most spectacular corners — as is the 160 mph Rindtcurve which finishes the long 3.7 mile
lap. The 190 miles Hungarian Grand Prix took two hours to run. The 192 miles Austrian race
would take under eighty minutes — when it eventually started.

With only a week between the two races all
the teams had travelled straight to Zeltweg
from Budapest to do their pre-race preparation at the circuit — mostly in a state of
relaxed calm. With their cars changed from
their 'high downforce' Hungaroring set-up to
the 'low downforce' Osterreichring specifica-
tion, the 26 drivers faced the first day of
practice on Friday with the knowledge that the

Styrian weather is notoriously unpredictable
— one minute clear blue skies and blazing
sunshine, the next glowering overcast and
pelting rain. So in Austria, more than anywhere, it pays to go for your grid time on
Friday and not assume that tomorrow, with a
day's testing behind you, you'll be able to go
quicker.

One man had an extra problem though —

All serene — but seconds later Stefan hit a deer at nearly 160 mph.

The 'second start' — total mayhem — miraculously
no-one was hurt.

Team Analysis

McLAREN

After three successive wins (Lauda, Prost, Prost) McLaren fail in Austria 1987. Prost, aiming for a hat-trick, qualifies ninth (slower than '85 and '86) with 'no power' and skittish rear end. Takes start three from pit lane after parade lap electrical problems. Races from 17th to 3rd (lap 31) but finishes sixth with instrument, misfire and boost problems. Johansson hits wandering deer at some 160 mph during Friday morning practice. Heavily involved in second start pile-up. Car destroyed. Starts race three in test car flown out from Woking Saturday evening. Lap two tyre stop. Right front wheel comes off on lap three (nut not tightened enough). Three wheels to pit. Then races to magnificent seventh, two laps down. Team still second in Championship but now seemingly hopeless 43 points behind Williams.

The Tyrrells of Palmer and Streiff after the first start crash — only Palmer started the real race.

TYRRELL

Palmer qualifies 24th with handling problems. Hit by Streiff at first start. Takes Start Two in spare car (giving AP carbon-fibre clutch its first race) and avoids pile-up. After third start finishes fourteenth (five laps down with limited revs due to broken valve spring) to further increase Class Championship lead. Streiff qualifies 25th. Hits Palmer at first start and severely damages second car at restart. With no cars left cannot take Start Three. Team Tyrrell now unbeatable in Colin Chapman 3½ litre Constructors' Championship.

WILLIAMS

Amidst incredible but strong rumours that team is to lose Japanese engines in 1988 Williams give Honda its 24th win in 100 races (and first ever finish in Austria). Mansell starts his 100th Grand Prix meeting (and seventh anniversary of his first GP drive: Austria 1980) by having wisdom tooth extracted Thursday evening. In great pain courageously qualifies second. Inadvertently causes Start Two pile-up as clutch slip delays getaway. After slow third start to preserve clutch catches and passes leader Piquet and takes magnificent fourth 1987 win with 150.5 mph record lap. Closes

Championship gap to Piquet to 15 points. Piquet hits Fabi exiting superfast Rindtcurve Friday morning practice. Takes fastest ever GP pole position at 160.2 mph. On day before 35th birthday settles for sixth second place of 1987 to retain Championship lead. With 43 point lead over McLaren, Williams looking unbeatable in Constructors' Championship.

BRABHAM

In excellent but underpowered chassis Patrese and de Cesaris qualify eighth and tenth after unusually trouble-free practice. Patrese, tipped for No. 2 Williams seat in '88, heavily involved in Start Two multiple crash. Takes third start in spare car. Retires from third place (engine: lap 44) having been fourth on lap 26. De Cesaris amazingly avoids both lap one accidents but again retires (eighth place: lap 36) with engine failure.

ZAKSPEED

Major modifications to car. Altered rear suspension, gearbox, differential, wings, turbos and electronic engine management chip. Happier Brundle qualifies 17th. Danner 20th. Brundle causes first 'Domino' multiple crash by losing car on notorious pit straight bump. Suspects drive shaft breakage. Again involved in second crash in spare car. In repaired spare car finishes fourteenth (four laps down) only to be disqualified for rear wing height rule infringement. Danner starts race three in repaired car after involvement in second accident. Finishes ninth, three laps down, unhappy with car's handling.

LOTUS

'Actively' suspended cars with major problems in Austria. Both Senna and Nakajima much concerned with practice handling and set-up problems. Senna starts 7th, Nakajima 13th (in spite of 1986 Formula 3000 race experience of Osterreichring). Senna takes third start from pit lane in spare car after breaking race car CV joint during second start. Stalls

But not for long!

Even Senna's Lotus won't fly without wings.

on grid. Races from 18th to 3rd (lap 25). After tyre stop rams obstructive Alboreto (lap 34) and removes front wings. Rejoins ninth with new set and improves to finish fifth by passing Prost on last of his 50 laps. Amidst strong rumours that joining McLaren in 1988 Senna still second Drivers' Championship but now only four points ahead of Mansell. Nakajima loses twelve places limping back to pits with tattered left rear tyre (lap 7). Rejoins 20th and lapped. Finishes 13th, three laps down, in fear of dismounted radio unit fouling pedals. Team Lotus, third in Constructors' Championship reduce gap to McLaren to two points.

AGS

Fabre qualifies last after potentially disastrous Friday practice Rindtcurve high speed contact with Piquet (Nelson's fault). Heavily involved in both start accidents. Takes third start in pit lane in spare car. Finishes 15th, last and unclassified, seven laps down.

MARCH

Excellent race for well-organised, cheerful and enthusiastic team. Capelli qualifies thirteenth. Savaged by Fabre's AGS in Start Two. Races to excellent eleventh (three laps down) in spare car to win atmospheric class with fastest 3½ litre lap.

ARROWS

Warwick, fully recovered from Hungary ailments, qualifies well at 11th. Avoids both start accidents. Races to sixth (lap 6) but slides to tenth (lap 34) with duff engine. Retires lap 36. Cheever qualifies twelfth despite failing boost. Takes first start in spare car (race car pick-up problem). Hit by Patrese and Johansson after re-start. Car severely damaged. Takes Start Three from pit lane in race car. Climbs from 20th to 9th (lap 25). Retires from 11th (lap 32) with rear tyre blowout.

BENETTON

At fast open Osterreichring, which suits Rory Byrne chassis (Berger and Fabi Benetton-BMWs first and second for 16 laps 1986), improved Ford engines using new fuel enable Boutsen and Fabi to take 4th and 5th grid places. Boutsen harries leader Piquet for fourteen laps. Pitstops lap 15 to correct gear linkage problem. Rejoins eleventh. Races to determined fourth (lapped) despite loose undertray and engine problems. Advances two places to seventh in Championship. Fabi improves to third, lap 15, but overshoots pit lap 21. Stops again lap 22. Rejoins seventh after jammed wheel nut

lengthens stop. Achieves best finish of year despite boost problems: third but lapped. Improves from 14th to 9th in Championship.

OSELLA

Another ghastly non-race for Caffi after qualifying 21st. Race car totalled at second start. Takes Start Three from pit lane. Retires at second corner, lap one, with electrical failure. Ninth non-finish from ten races.

MINARDI

The usual grey day for Minardi who, after Austria had only had one finish from twenty 1987 driver-starts. Nannini qualifies 15th, Campos 19th. Campos clouts Arnoux Start One. Hurtles round in eleventh lap one. Improves to tenth lap two but retires lap four (electrics). Nannini in other Minardi hits Arnoux Start Three. Retires lap two (engine).

LIGIER

Team effort greatly reduced by having only five Megatron engines for entire meeting. Very limited practice for both drivers. Arnoux starts 16th, Ghinzani 18th. Arnoux severely affected by 'Minarditis' (hit by Campos Start One and Nannini Start Three!) Overcomes resultant bent steering arm penalty to finish tenth, three laps down. Ghinzani crashes race car Start One and spare Start Two. Uses repaired race car for Start Three to finish eighth, two laps down. Team announce intention to use John Judd Honda V8 atmospheric engines in new 1988 car.

FERRARI

Another strong start. Another 'no points' finish (fifth in a row). Berger, after treatment by Willi Dungl, fit after Hungary malaise. Starts excellent third. After running third dishearteningly retires from 4th place lap 6 (turbo). Alboreto qualifies 6th. After furiously berating FISA President Jean-Marie Ballestre about Osterreichring inadequacies following Start Two even more furiously takes Start Three from pit lane after pits visit to correct misaligned steering wheel. Races brilliantly from 19th to 3rd (lap 23). Drops to 7th lap 42 (loss of boost). Retires lap 43.

LOLA

Alliot again qualifies fastest of 'Atmospherics' (22nd). Involved in Start Two fracas. Races spare car to 12th, three laps down.

But where was the man with the Chequered Flag when Nigel Mansell won?

Nigel Mansell. On Thursday evening an abscess that had been increasingly bothering him reached a high point of unpleasantness. So, with a local anaesthetic, out came a wisdom tooth to leave a gaping, bleeding and really painful hole in Nigel's head. But, undaunted, and with typical determination, he rocketed round the 'Ring in 1 minute 23.46 seconds — faster than Teo Fabi's 1986 pole time in the Benetton-BMW. So that was Nigel's eighth pole of 1987? No! With just twelve minutes to go — too late for Mansell to stop his full-tank testing, pump out some forty gallons of fuel, and go for a faster lap — Nelson Piquet went 1/10 of a second quicker to achieve the fastest-ever qualifying lap speed in the history of Grand Prix racing — 160.2 miles an hour.

But overshadowing Piquet's achievement, the faces in the paddock reflected people's horror at Stefan Johansson's appalling accident. Breasting the wooded rise approaching the Rindtcurve at some 160 miles an hour he saw a deer on the track immediately ahead of him. No way to avoid the unfortunate animal at that speed. Swerve — but straight in. Instant carnage. Immediate death for the poor beast and a totally destroyed McLaren. Mira-

culously though, an unharmed Johansson except for shock, bruises and stiffness.

But, with the failure to stop practice after the deer had been seen at least ten minutes earlier, the failure even to show warning flags and the amused indifference of the marshals as they watched eager spectators take 'souvenirs' from Stefan's shattered McLaren, this was a major indication that all was not well at the Osterreichring. More was to come.

On Saturday morning it rained. And rained. And rained. After lunch a dry line started to appear with about ten minutes of the qualifying session to go but by then it was too late. Nobody got near their Friday time — some didn't even bother to go out. So it was another Williams front row — the fourth of the year — with Piquet on pole ahead of Mansell. Berger's Ferrari a promising third (with Gerhard rid of his Hungary 'flu after two days with Niki Lauda's personal physician Willi Dungl) followed by the Benetton-Fords of Boutsen and Fabi. Alboreto sixth and Senna seventh ('Active' suspension seemingly not yet in tune with the high speed bumps in Austria). World Champion Alain Prost, the man who'd won the Austrian GP in 1983, '85 and '86, was down in ninth place — 'No power and the rear end won't stick'.

Race day weather was as good as Saturday's had been bad. At 14.30 they departed with the usual blood-tingling blaze of colour and blast of noise with Boutsen to a determined second ahead of Mansell and Berger. But chaos behind them as Martin Brundle's Zakspeed hit the infamous bump at the bottom of the pits-straight hill, snapped sideways, hit the armco and bounced back across the track. So narrow is the straight that there was nowhere for those behind him to go except into something solid. Which they did. Streiff into Palmer. Campos into Arnoux. Ghinzani into the armco.

That was Start One. Forty minutes later, in repaired or spare cars they tried again — amazingly all 26 of them. This time the chaos was down to Mansell as a slipping clutch made him a mobile chicane and the second start a dodgems shambles. Nearly half the grid involved. Johansson, Streiff, Patrese, Brundle, Danner, Senna, Fabi, Capelli, Cheever, Caffi, Ghinzani and Alliot! Twelve broken cars but nobody hurt. Astounding.

One and three-quarter hours after the first start the Austrian Grand Prix got underway. With 25 cars starting — six of them from the pit lane! An unwanted Grand Prix record, with a car-less Streiff gloomily sitting this one out in the pits. But after an incident-packed two days of practice (and no practice) and two mega-shambles of starts the spirited race was almost a rest cure for everyone's jangled nerves.

With Mansell easing his Williams gently into its third start of the day to preserve its suspect clutch Piquet just led Boutsen for fourteen inspiring laps with the multi-coloured Benetton at times right on his gearbox. A thoroughly fed-up Berger, third for three laps, was out on lap six (turbo again) and on lap 15 Mansell was second and Fabi (Benetton) third as the unhappy Boutsen stopped to have a sloppy gear-linkage fixed.

Lap 21: Mansell daringly sliced past Piquet and there he stayed in his 100th Grand Prix, to win his fourth of the year and just about keep his Championship hopes alive in a race which ran an extra lap when the man with the chequred flag failed to see Nigel cross the line! Third black mark Austria. With Piquet

settling for six points from his sixth second place of the season it was another fruitless race for Alboreto who slipped from a brilliant third to seventh and out of the race (his seventh 1987 retirement) on lap 43 with a loss of boost.

But if the Ferraris failed again the Benettons didn't. In spite of their many and varied troubles (see 'Team Analysis') they were, in the words of Designer Rory Byrne, 'really competitive for the first time this year' finishing third (Fabi) and fourth to the all-conquering Williams.

Glorious grandeur of Styria — a marvellous backcloth for Alboreto and Streiff.

Austria, though, seemed to have effectively ended the Championship aspirations of Senna and Prost. With the Lotus again failing to reproduce its Monaco and Detroit winning form it seemed unlikely that the team would be able to sharpen up enough to enable Ayrton to improve on his second place in the Championship in the six races that were left. As for Prost, who raced up to third from the pit lane by lap 31, but who then slid to sixth beset by boost and electrical problems, sadly said 'I must now admit, I think, that I will not be this year's Champion.'

So who would it be? Piquet for the third time? Or Mansell for the first? 'Now,' said Nelson, 'I can take chances like Nigel and go for wins.' But with Nigel saying to me in the TV interview room 'I intend to win the next six races,' it looked as though Grand Prix enthusiasts were in for an exciting time!

Either way, with incredible rumours circulating that the Williams team were to lose their Honda engines in 1988, Frank's men had given their power-suppliers something to think about!

You don't look a day over 33 Nigel! Mr Mansell celebrates his 100th Grand Prix.

AUSTRIAN GRAND PRIX

Winner: Nigel Mansell, Williams FW11B/3 **Fastest Lap:** Nigel Mansell, 150.531 mph

GRID POSITION		RESULTS			WORLD CHAMPIONSHIP				
No.	Driver	Pos.	Driver	Car	Drivers	Pts	Constructors		Pts
6	Piquet	1	Mansell	Williams-Honda FW11B/3	1. Piquet	54	1. Williams-Honda		93
5	Mansell	2	Piquet	Williams-Honda FW11B/4	2. Senna	43	2. McLaren-TAG		50
28	Berger	3	Fabi	Benetton-Ford B187-07	3. Mansell	39	3. Lotus-Honda		49
20	Boutsen	4	Boutsen	Benetton-Ford B187-06	4. Prost	31	4. Ferrari		17
19	Fabi	5	Senna	Lotus-Honda 99T/6	5. Johansson	19	5. Benetton-Ford		15
27	Alboreto	6	Prost	McLaren-TAG MP4/3-4	6. Berger	9	6. Tyrrell-Cosworth		8
12	Senna	7	Johansson	McLaren-TAG MP4/3-3	7. Alboreto	8	7. Arrows-Megatron		7
7	Patrese	8	Ghinzani	Ligier-Megatron JS29C-5	Boutsen	8	8. Brabham-BMW		6
1	Prost	9	Danner	Zakspeed 871/2	9. Fabi	7	9. Zakspeed		2
8	De Cesaris	10	Arnoux	Ligier-Megatron JS29C-5	10. Nakajima	6	10. Ligier-Megatron		1
17	Warwick	11	Capelli	March-Cosworth 871/03	11. Cheever	4	Lola-Cosworth		1
18	Cheever	12	Alliot	Lola-Cosworth LC87/02	De Cesaris	4	March-Cosworth		1
11	Nakajima	13	Nakajima	Lotus-Honda 99T/5	Palmer	4			
2	Johansson	14	Palmer	Tyrrell-Cosworth DG016-6	Streiff	4			
24	Nannini				15. Warwick	3			
25	Arnoux				16. Brundle	2			
9	Brundle				Patrese	2			
26	Ghinzani				18. Alliot	1			
23	Campos				Arnoux	1			
10	Danner				Capelli	1			
21	Caffi								
30	Alliot				**JIM CLARK CUP**		**COLIN CHAPMAN CUP**		
16	Capelli				1. Palmer	61	1. Tyrrell-Cosworth		106
3	Palmer				2. Streiff	45	2. AGS-Cosworth		35
4	Streiff				3. Fabre	35	3. Lola-Cosworth		25
14	Fabre				4. Alliot	25	4. March-Cosworth		19
					5. Capelli	19			

6th September 1987
Circuit: Monza

THE Italian Grand Prix is usually something special. It certainly was this year. First of all there is its location. Monza, situated in the Royal Park on the outskirts of Milan, is the oldest Grand Prix circuit in current use. Built in 1922 its 3.6 mile, 155 mph, lap may have had three chicanes inserted to slow it down but it is basically the same now as it was 65 years ago and it absolutely oozes tradition and history. Only at Monza can you walk around and say to yourself 'Nuvolari raced against Varzi here. Caracciola and Rosemeyer fought for victory here in their Mercedes-Benz and Auto-Union. Ascari father and Ascari son raced for Alfa-Romeo and Ferrari here.' Indeed it was at Monza that the brilliant Alberto lost his life. Every driver and car of Grand Prix note has competed at Monza and you really feel it in the atmosphere. Add to that the passionate raceday enthusiasm of over 100,000 Ferrari-loving 'Tifosi', those Italian super-enthusiasts, and you have an unrivalled recipe for a memorable Grand Prix experience!

But Monza 1987 had extra ingredients to spice the heady mix. Confirmation of the two major rumours that had been circulating in the Grand Prix world for weeks. McLaren were to replace their tremendously successful Porsche-designed and built TAG engines with Honda power in 1988 — at the expense of Williams. And Ayrton Senna had signed a three year contract to join Alain Prost in the McLaren team next season — which meant that Stefan Johansson had to find himself a new seat for '88.

After their four victorious seasons with Williams (twenty wins with, doubtless, more to come) the Grand Prix world found Honda's move baffling. But the inscrutable Japanese, who had allegedly paid all of Nelson Piquet's massive $3.3 million retainer at Williams, plus the team's enormous testing costs, appeared to feel that, in giving Piquet and Mansell equal cars and support instead of favouring the Brazilian, Williams had failed to honour the terms of their contract. And they were clearly annoyed by the independence that the team had shown in refusing to accept Honda's suggestion that Satoru Nakajima should be their second driver in 1987. So, with the TAG engine now experiencing consistency problems, Williams' loss was to be McLaren's gain. It's a hard world in Grand Prix racing.

1988, with major driver and engine changes (Williams to use the British Judd atmospheric 3½ litre V8 motor in company with Ligier and March) was obviously going to be full of interest and excitement. But this was 1987, and Williams generated another major talking point — Nelson Piquet was to use their 'Active' suspension at Monza for the first time. All season Frank Dernie, the team's aerodynamicist, had been quietly developing a Williams 'Active' system (more hydraulic-based than the far more sophisticated Lotus electronics-oriented set-up) and now it was ready to race. Nelson Piquet was not only very

Ayrton Senna getting ready.

93

Nelson spectacular in practice — he didn't make a mistake in the race.

De Cesaris' car smoking grass.

enthusiastic about it, but had done all the testing. Mansell, biased against 'Active' suspension by a multitude of hair-raising 'adventures' he had experienced with the early Lotus developments, had avoided having anything to do with it. A situation which he was to regret, because on Saturday evening, after the usual two days of practice in hot and humid conditions, a delighted Nelson Piquet knew that when the grid formed on Sunday he would be occupying his third pole position of 1987 and the twenty-third of his outstanding career. Piquet and Mansell, in his 'conventional' Williams, had had a thrilling duel for pole, with first one and then the other taking it. Piquet's time of one minute 23.46 seconds (155.45 mph) was a mere ⅒th second faster than Mansell's. Enough though! But Mansell was again in the front row as he had been for every race of the year — a superb achievement.

To the unbridled delight of the 'Tifosi' Gerhard Berger's Ferrari was a very strong third on the grid with a time faster than Teo Fabi's 1986 pole position. And although Michele Alboreto was to start from eighth place his scarlet F187 had been as quick as Berger's until a forceful introduction to the armco had deranged it. With Senna's Lotus, Prost's McLaren and the Benettons of Boutsen and Fabi occupying the fourth to seventh places and covered by ⅒th of a second things looked good for a dramatic race!

Which is exactly what the 1987 Italian Grand Prix turned out to be. Dramatic and exciting. Right down to the last lap.

Three men started it still very much in contention for the World Championship. Piquet (54 points). Senna (43). And Mansell (39). 'But Mansell hasn't got a chance' said the cynics. 'Can you see Honda letting him win now that they and Senna are going to McLaren and Piquet is going to Honda-powered Lotus next year? Nigel's had it.' Hardly a charitable view but one seemingly supported by the strange Monza statement by Honda's boss of Formula One, Yoshitoshi Sakurai, that 'our drivers' engies are identical although we can and do make adjustments to compensate for their different driving styles.'

With the parade lap finished and seconds to go pandemonium reigned. Patrese's Brabham was on fire. Or seemed to be. It was vapour from the fuel-tank breather actually but, as the fire marshals descended on it, and with a mass of yellow flags furiously waving, the FISA starter Roland Bruynseraede commendably withheld the green light. Minutes later with no damage done, with another parade lap completed and with the race distance reduced from 51 to 50 laps they were off.

A superb getaway by Mansell took him into the lead — for about two hundred metres — before he was passed by Piquet. With the knowledge that Nelson's new suspension system enabled him to have a lower ride height and more downforce but less drag and, therefore, lower fuel consumption, Mansell had to try to break clear and build a cushion between himself and Piquet. But he never even remotely looked like doing so. Second for one lap he was passed first by Boutsen and then by Berger after he'd banged wheels with the Ferrari on lap two. Eventually he passed them both and even briefly challenged Piquet for second after Nelson's tyre stop. But, in finishing third, Monza brought no joy to Mansell — with a twenty point gap between himself and his team-mate, his Championship chances appeared to have disappeared.

Boutsen and Berger had a marvellous scrap

But Michele Alboreto's 100th Grand Prix — on his home circuit too — was not to be a happy one. Retirement on lap fourteen after he'd hit a kerb, displaced his undertray, lost his sidepod and caused a turbo to expire. And nor was Alain Prost to achieve that elusive record 28th Grand Prix win which had looked so easily attainable after he had equalled Jackie Stewart's 27 victories in Belgium. McLaren arrived at Monza thinking that four days of testing at Imola had cured their Bosch electronics problem. But it hadn't. With his engine again infuriatingly cutting in and out

Senna's gamble to use only one set of tyres ultimately cost him the race.

for second with the Belgian, supremely happy with his Benetton's balance and his Ford engine's power, repeating the form he'd shown in Austria. Second for fourteen laps at the Osterreichring. Second for twenty-two laps at Monza. With Berger on his gearbox for sixteen of them. Mansell fourth. Prost fifth. Senna sixth and Alboreto seventh pursued by Johansson.

Alain was into the pits initially from fifth, and then from a dispiriting ninth place for inspection and, hopefully, correction. He got going and, typically, never gave up — even breaking the lap record. But he finished fifteenth, four laps down, his World Championship hat-trick now effectively a broken dream.

Not many people noticed Prost's plight though — all eyes were on the absorbing

Team Analysis

McLAREN

Team arrive at Monza optimistic after Imola tests to correct handling and engine management problems. Press conference confirms that in 1988, McLaren will use Honda engines and Senna will replace Johansson. Prost, unable to match rivals' engine power, qualifies fifth and Johansson eleventh. Prost, plagued by repetition of engine cutting out problems, slides to ninth. Pits lap ten to change black box. Rejoins last to finish fifteenth four laps down. Still fourth in championship but now only mathematically in contention. Johansson, with strapped ribs after Austria crash, races to sixth place despite handling, brake, rev-limiter and electronic problems. After disappointing race team lose second place in Constructors Championship to Lotus. Arrival optimism clearly misplaced.

TYRRELL

3½ litre Atmospheric engined cars severely disadvantaged at Monza power circuit. (Seven seconds a lap off the pace.) Palmer qualifies 22nd and fastest in class. Affected by heavy oversteer in race. Finishes fourteenth overall and third in class, three laps down, to retain class Championship lead. Streiff starts 24th in new chassis. Drives sturdy race to twelfth overall and class win, three laps down.

WILLIAMS

Honda and team confirm that Williams lose Honda engines in 1988. British Judd VA atmospheric 3½ litre motor to replace Honda power. Piquet practises and races new 'Active' suspension car for first time. Takes third pole position of season — faster than Fabi 1986 time. Leads race until lap 24 tyre stop. Rejoins second behind non-stop Senna. Retakes lead when Senna goes off (lap 43). Wins third GP of year and increases Championship lead. Mansell, in conventional-suspension car, occupies grid front-row position (second) for twelfth consecutive GP. Clouts kerb lap two and drops to fourth. Fights back to second lap 19. After tyre stop lap 21 unable to catch non-stop Senna and finishes distant third with overheating engine. Retains Championship third place with increased gap to leader Piquet (20 points). Team Williams now only mathematically beatable in Constructors Championship.

No joy for Patrese in his home Grand Prix — Berger behind finished a fine fourth.

BRABHAM

Patrese, strongly tipped to join Williams in 1988, qualifies strong ninth. Causes first start to be aborted due to ignition of fuel-tank breather vapour. Retires lap six when eleventh (blown engine). De Cesaris starts tenth. Retains place until lap eight retirement (broken front upright). Rumours continue that Brabham, a shadow of its former self, being sold or terminated at end of season.

ZAKSPEED

Post-Austria Nurburgring testing effects further improvements. New engine frame, differential, suspension geometry and turbo inlets. Brundle impressed but, with motor problems, qualifies 17th. Races to excellent eighth but obliged to withdraw, lap 43, with disintegrating gearbox. Danner starts 16th. Delayed by jammed wheel nut at lap 26 tyre stop. Nevertheless finishes encouraging ninth, two laps down.

LOTUS

With good 'Active' suspension set-up Senna (who joins McLaren in 1988) qualifies fourth. Surprises rivals with

'Turbo' Piquet versus 'Atmospheric' Capelli — no contest.

non-stop race. Takes lead lap 24 but goes off, lap 43, when passing Ghinzani Ligier. Loses lead to Piquet but recovers brilliantly to finish second, 1.8 seconds down, with record lap of 149.48 mph. Retains Championship second place fourteen points behind Piquet. Nakajima qualifies 14th. Goes off lap four. Rejoins last. Finishes eleventh, three laps down. Team Lotus improve to second in Constructors Championship.

AGS

With the appearance of two extra entries (Osella and Coloni) Pascal Fabre fails to qualify.

MARCH

Team confirms its intention to use Judd 3½ litre V8 atmospheric engines in 1988 two-car team. Capelli qualifies 25th using Hart prepared Ford-Cosworth DFZ engine for first time. Finishes 13th, three laps down, and second in class with acute understeer.

ARROWS

Derek Warwick qualifies well at twelfth. Moves up to tenth in race benefiting from two Brabham retirements. Retires lap ten (metering unit). Cheever starts 13th. Races strongly to eighth lap 14. Holds place until lap 26 retirement (CV joint).

Alliot returns with seat — the crowd had the car.

BENETTON

Encouraging car reliability improvement maintained in Italy. Boutsen and Fabi qualify strong sixth and seventh. Boutsen opportunely seizes second place lap two. Impressively retains it until lap 23 tyre stop. Delayed thereafter by loose undertray and high fuel consumption but finishes fifth. Fabi, troubled by lack of grip throughout race, finishes seventh (lapped). A good race for Benetton.

Franco Forini still saving for the contact lenses.

OSELLA

Second car entered for Swiss driver Franco Forini, 1985 Italian F3 Champion, who does well to qualify 26th in aged car. Circulates at back of field in first GP until inevitable retirement lap 23 (turbo). Caffi qualifies 21st. Retires from fourteenth lap 16 (suspension).

MINARDI

Campos starts 20th. Retires lap 35 (engine fire) when sixteenth. Nannini qualifies 18th and runs steady race only, to run out of fuel when sixteenth lap 46.

LIGIER

Major disagreement with Heini Mader, the Swiss supplier of team's Megatron engines, results in both cars failing to appear in Saturday timed practice. Arnoux and Ghinzani nevertheless qualify 15th and 19th with Friday times. Surprisingly good race for both men. Ghinzani finishes eighth and Arnoux tenth, both two laps down.

FERRARI

Slow but steady John Barnard-inspired car improvements continue. Berger qualifies excellent third using rebuilt car crashed by Alboreto in practice. In contention against Williams, Benetton and Lotus rivals all through race. Finishes fourth. Alboreto qualifies eighth in down-on-power spare car after practice crash in race car. Improves to sixth lap eight but loses left side-pod which causes overheating followed by turbo failure. Retires lap 14.

LOLA

Alliot, 23rd on grid. Races against Streiff improving to 13th lap 28. Retires lap 38 after collision with Streiff Tyrrell at Parabolica.

COLONI

New conventional 3½ litre Ford-Cosworth powered Italian car entered by ex race driver Enzo Coloni for Nicola Larini, 1986 F3 Champion of Italy. Teething problems adversely affect performance. Larini fails to qualify.

battle for the lead. Piquet, revelling in the benefits of his 'Active' suspension, held it comfortably until his lap 23 tyre stop when Senna, who'd charged past first Mansell and then Berger and Boutsen when they stopped for fresh rubber, took over the number one position. Piquet rejoined the race in second place on lap 24. No problem. He'd retake the lead when Senna stopped.

But as Ayrton reeled off lap after lap with a steady ten second lead it became clear that he wasn't going to. 'I knew I'd never beat Piquet if I stopped. So I decided to go on if I could. It was win or nothing — I had to beat Nelson.' On the car-to-pit radio he told his Team Manager Peter Warr he wanted to stay out if the tyres would stand it. The Goodyear technicians said it would be marginal but Senna decided to go for a non-stop run — as he had when he'd won in Detroit. And it seemed to have been an inspired decision. Lap 40 — ten to go — Senna led by 4½ seconds brilliantly conserving his tyres as Piquet, blistering his and suffering from the

resultant vibration, strove to close the gap. Lap 43 and Nelson had done so — now he was only 2½ seconds behind Senna.

With seven laps to go to a magnificent victory Senna tried to put Ghinzani's Ligier between himself and Piquet's Williams as he braked for the 160 mph, 180 degree, Parabolica bend. In doing so he got on to the 'dirty' inside line, lost the Lotus and shot off the track into the sand trap. Amazingly he had the presence of mind not only to accelerate to avoid digging-in but subsequently to dab the brakes to shoot the debris out of his side pods when he rejoined the track!

Now in second place behind Piquet, Senna's driving for the remaining eight laps was awesome. With his car amazingly undamaged but with his tyres now on the ragged edge he charged. Two and a half seconds ahead Piquet broke the lap record on lap 49 to preserve his lead. Senna smashed it on the last lap (1 minute 26.8 seconds, 149.48 mph) to finish 1.8 seconds behind Piquet. A tremendous race —

12 men — 8 seconds — 4 new Goodyears.

Monza — cars, crowds,
fanaticism, flags and girls.

Nelson's 20th win and a superb first for the Williams 'Active' suspension.

Mansell finished third (in spite of reduced power due to an overheating engine — 'What did we tell you?' said the cynics) after grittily catching and passing Berger's Ferrari. Gerhard took his fourth fourth-place of '87 ahead of Boutsen, who'd had to slow an excellent drive with a broken undertray and fuel consumption problems, whilst Johansson finished sixth to earn a single point even though his TAG engine rev-limiter hadn't been limiting.

If a Ferrari couldn't win the 'Tifosi' wanted it to be a Brazilian. So it was some consolation that they had both of them to cheer — and they did so. In their wildly excited thousands. Piquet first. Senna second. And one of them now seemingly certain to be the Honda-powered World Champion.

With Mansell's Williams-Honda third Yoshitoshi Sakurai must have felt it had been a good race.

Well done Piquet San! But next year no Nelson and no Honda for Williams.

ITALIAN GRAND PRIX

Winner: Nelson Piquet, Williams FW11B/5   *Fastest Lap:* Ayrton Senna, 149.479 mph

GRID POSITION		RESULTS		
No.	Driver	Pos. Driver	Car	
6	Piquet	1 Piquet	Williams-Honda FW11B/5	
5	Mansell	2 Senna	Lotus-Honda 99T/3	
28	Berger	3 Mansell	Williams-Honda FW11B/3	
12	Senna	4 Berger	Ferrari F187/097	
1	Prost	5 Boutsen	Benetton-Ford B187-07	
20	Boutsen	6 Johansson	McLaren-TAG MP4/3-5	
19	Fabi	7 Fabi	Benetton-Ford B187-04	
27	Alboreto	8 Ghinzani	Ligier-Megatron JS29C/04	
7	Patrese	9 Danner	Zakspeed 871/02	
8	De Cesaris	10 Arnoux	Ligier-Megatron JS29C/05	
2	Johansson	11 Nakajima	Lotus-Honda 99T/3	
17	Warwick	12 Streiff	Tyrrell-Cosworth DG/016-7	
18	Cheever	13 Capelli	March-Cosworth 871/2	
11	Nakajima	14 Palmer	Tyrrell-Cosworth DG/016-6	
25	Arnoux	15 Prost	McLaren-TAG MP4/3-4	
10	Danner	16 Nannini	Minardi-Moderni M186/2	
9	Brundle			
24	Nannini			
26	Ghinzani			
23	Campos			
21	Caffi			
3	Palmer			
30	Alliot			
4	Streiff			
16	Capelli			
22	Forini			

WORLD CHAMPIONSHIP

Drivers		Pts	Constructors		Pts
1.	Piquet	63	1.	Williams-Honda	106
2.	Senna	49	2.	Lotus-Honda	55
3.	Mansell	43	3.	McLaren-TAG	51
4.	Prost	31	4.	Ferrari	20
5.	Johansson	20	5.	Benetton-Ford	17
6.	Berger	12	6.	Tyrrell-Cosworth	8
7.	Boutsen	10	7.	Arrows-Megatron	7
8.	Alboreto	8	8.	Brabham-BMW	6
9.	Fabi	7	9.	Zakspeed	2
10.	Nakajima	6	10.	Ligier-Megatron	1
11.	Cheever	4		Lola-Cosworth	1
	De Cesaris	4		March-Cosworth	1
	Palmer	4			
	Streiff	4			
15.	Warwick	3			
16.	Brundle	2			
	Patrese	2			
18.	Alliot	1			
	Arnoux	1			
	Capelli	1			

JIM CLARK CUP			COLIN CHAPMAN CUP		
1.	Palmer	65	1.	Tyrrell-Cosworth	119
2.	Streiff	54	2.	AGS-Cosworth	35
3.	Fabre	35	3.	Lola-Cosworth	25
4.	Alliot	25		March-Cosworth	25
	Capelli	25			

PORTUGAL

20th September 1987
Circuit: Estoril

SATURDAY, 19th September, 13.28 hours. With rain clouds threatening the superb but bumpy Estoril Autodrome Gerhard Berger swept into the pit lane for a set of new pre-heated Goodyear slicks. Straight out and into a build-up lap. Then, with his tyres at their peak, a lap which eclipsed the opposition. One minute 17.62 seconds (125.36 mph). Brilliant timing as, seconds later, a light shower lubricated the track and a Ferrari was in pole position for the first time since Brazil, 1985. Ferrari were out of the doldrums and back in contention!

Portugal is a comparative newcomer to the Grand Prix scene; this was to be only the fourth Formula One race on the Estoril circuit. 2.7 miles long, it is situated in a rocky valley a few kilometres from the most westerly point in Europe — the spectacular Cabo da Roca which looks, uninterrupted, across the Atlantic to America. And it's a circuit which the drivers like — lots of corners, a couple of 200 mph straights and a vital need to get a good balance on the car. That, plus uphill and downhill gradient as the track swoops round the valley sides makes it a real test of driving ability. It's a circuit too that, in its short Grand Prix life has seen some memorable races: 1984 when Alain Prost won the Grand Prix but lost the World Championship to his team mate Niki Lauda by half a point. 1985 when Ayrton Senna brilliantly won his first Grand Prix in torrential rain. And 1986 when Nigel Mansell dominated from start to finish.

With Alain Prost seemingly out of the World Championship 1987, Portugal was going to be critical to Piquet, Senna and Mansell the top three contenders and another win would surely give Nelson his third world title. All the top teams had been testing since the Italian GP — McLaren at Monza in an effort to overcome their engine management problems, Williams at Brands Hatch to give Nigel Mansell experience of their 'Active' suspension which had enabled Nelson Piquet to win in Italy and Ferrari at Fiorano to hone their ever-improving F187.

Their efforts were soon to reward the waiting world with a historic race that will be talked about for years to come.

The two days of practising and qualifying were hot, humid and sticky with an ever-present threat of rain. And they showed us how well Ferrari had painstakingly developed

Nelson Piquet proudly sporting the new ICI logo whilst finishing third in spite of jointly causing the 'first' race stoppage.

their beautiful 187 which looked superb but which had consistently failed to live up to its visual promise. Technical Director John Barnard, whose demanding standards had made him a far from popular man at Ferrari, had done a grand job with the help of his colleagues — especially aerodynamicist and suspension man Harvey Postlethwaite. More power — and reliable power — from the V6 turbo engine and vastly improved handling had transformed the 187's track performance. Berger topped two of the four practice ses-

101

sions and was number one on the grid whilst Alboreto, although delayed by gearbox problems, was well on the pace too.

So, as the 26 car grid formed up for the 70 lap, 189.2 miles, race at two-thirty on Sunday afternoon the 'Prancing Horse' of Maranello was riding high. Berger in his first-ever pole position. Mansell next (his thirteenth consecutive front row place) and Alain Prost back at the front in third position — well pleased with both the power and the handling of his McLaren. Then Nelson Piquet, followed by Senna (in spite of handling problems and an engine bay fire on Saturday), Alboreto, Patrese, Johansson and the Benettons of Boutsen and Fabi.

But then the bad news. For the third Grand Prix in succession a shambles at the start. At the very first corner a multiple pile-up involv-

ing Warwick, Nakajima, Brundle, Danner, Campos, Arnoux, Alliot and Cheever which had been triggered by a coming-together between Piquet and Alboreto. Ten of the 26 starters in immediate trouble as the race was stopped — albeit, and to the deep shame of the organisers, not until the second lap. With cars and debris still on the circuit as the remaining runners, led by Berger and Mansell, swept into their second lap it was a miracle that there was not a major disaster. Forty minutes later, with the wrecks retrieved, with Alboreto, Brundle, Alliot, Arnoux and Cheever in their spare cars, with the unfortunate Christian Danner having no Zakspeed to compete in and with Campos and Palmer starting from the pit lane the 1987 Portuguese Grand Prix got successfully under way.

As they streamed past the pits it was Mansell

Christian Danner gloomily surveys Brundle's Zakspeed — his was worse.

Arnoux removes his seat for his spare car — he broke that one too.

in front but on lap two Berger confidently took his Ferrari into a lead which he progressively built to over ten seconds. Behind him a superb scrap, with Mansell heading Senna, Piquet, Prost, Alboreto and Boutsen until lap five when Alboreto, looking as relaxed and assured as his team-mate, took fifth from Prost.

Lap eleven and Piquet, not totally at ease with his Williams which had had to have a new nosecone and a suspension check after his first-start collision, moved up to third past Senna as Teo Fabi's Benetton, now eighth, started to motor.

But Senna, the darling of the very pro-Brazilian Portuguese crowd, was in trouble with wildly fluctuating engine revs due to a faulty electronic sensor. Down to seventh and then into the pits for a new control box — a long stop which saw him rejoin last but one, three laps down, to start a magnificent but fruitless fight to get back into the points.

On lap 14 though an even more dramatic

development. Nigel Mansell out! Delighted with the race handling of his 'Active' suspension Williams he had been having no trouble in keeping ahead of Piquet and Senna and was catching Berger when suddenly 'the engine went on to three or four cylinders as I came past the pits.' And that was it. Mansell's second successive race marred by an engine problem and his fifth retirement of the season. 'Told you Honda wouldn't let him do well,' said the cynics.

So now, at one-third distance, lap 23, with Senna and Mansell out of the frame, it was a supremely confident Gerhard Berger leading with Piquet second, Alboreto up to third — and charging — Prost fourth, Fabi fifth and De Cesaris driving an excellent race in sixth place. And the unfortunate Thierry Boutsen, who had been fifth for lap after lap, into the pits for a long fault-finding stop (broken plug electrode).

With no disrespect to the season-long supremacy of Williams and McLaren it had

Team Analysis

Prost's relentless and brilliant pursuit of Berger —
motor racing at its best.

McLAREN

Magnificent victorious return for team after recent comparative lack of success. Engine electronics problems solved at post-Italian GP Monza testing session. Prost qualifies third. Races to second on lap 39. Relentlessly pursues race leader Berger — both on failing tyres. Pressures Berger into spin lap 68 and brilliantly wins record 28th Grand Prix at record speed. Remains fourth in Championship now with mathematical if remote chance of third successive win. Johansson qualifies eighth and finishes excellent fifth with major handling problems caused by understeer and broken front wheel bearing. Retains Championship fifth place. Team return to second place in Constructors Championship as welcome result of return to top form (first '87 win since Belgian GP).

TYRRELL

Ken Tyrrell's 'Atmospheric' team welcome end of 1987 super-fast circuits with return to slower Estoril venue. Ken personally engineers Streiff car. Palmer starts from pit lane due to electrical problem on second grid after qualifying 24th. Grittily drives to excellent tenth overall and second in class one-fifth of a second behind class winner Capelli. Retains commanding lead in 3½ litre class Drivers Championship. Streiff qualifies 21st (second in class). Finishes twelfth on heavily worn tyres after spin.

WILLIAMS

In his first major test of 'Active' Williams at post-Italian GP Brands Hatch session Mansell breaks lap record. Team take four cars to Estoril. One 'Active' and one 'passive' for each driver. Mansell qualifies second and takes thirteenth successive front row grid position in 'Active' car. Leads lap one. Races comfortable and challenging second behind Berger until lap 14 when retires with electronics problem. Retains Drivers Championship third place with reduced mathematical chance of winning. Piquet hits Alboreto Ferrari after first start. Punctures front tyre and damages nosecone. Benefits from race stoppage to start race two in restored 'Active' car. Finishes third (lowest scoring 1987 race position so far!) and increases Championship lead over Senna to 18 points.

BRABHAM

Patrese qualifies seventh. Retires lap 14 with major engine failure when ninth. De Cesaris starts thirteenth. Improves to sixth lap 31. After excellent drive has misfortune to retire lap 55 with injection problem.

ZAKSPEED

Martin Brundle starts 50th GP from 17th on grid. Heavily involved with first lap multiple collision. Drives strongly to tenth place lap 23. Retires lap 36 (gearbox). Danner starts race one sixteenth. Car irreparably damaged in first lap multiple collision. Does not start race two as Brundle in spare car.

LOTUS
Team bothered by 'Active' suspension problems and engine bay fires in both cars during practice. Nakajima qualifies 15th for first race at Estoril. Involved with Brundle Zakspeed in race one collision. Finishes non-stop race two in eighth place, two laps down. Senna qualifies fifth after practice handling problems. Suffers engine electronic sensor failure in race necessitating long stop to change control box. After dropping to 22nd (last but one) for eight laps fights back to finish outstanding, but no-points, seventh, two laps down. Retains championship second place with increased gap (18 points) to leader Piquet. Team Lotus lose recently gained Constructors Championship second place to McLaren.

AGS
Pascal Fabre again fails to qualify. Badly needed new car being built for 1988 with French regional government backing.

MARCH
After qualifying 22nd (third in class) Ivan Capelli drives outstanding race to finish ninth overall and win 3½ litre category for the second time in three races by finishing one-fifth of a second ahead of inspired Jonathan Palmer. Team now only one point behind slow but consistent AGS in Colin Chapman 'atmospheric' Constructors Championship.

ARROWS
Team reliability benefiting from sufficient sponsorship to permit between-races testing. Derek Warwick qualifies twelfth and is involved in race one multiple collision incident. After long delay caused by spinning off circuit in race two (locking brake) finishes 13th, four laps down. Excellent race for Cheever despite starting race two from eleventh on grid in spare car after having been hit by Warwick following first start. Advances to sixth, lap 54, and stays there to score single championship point, two laps down. Team well pleased with both cars still running at race end.

Eddie Cheever — sixth in the pretty Ross Brawn Arrows.

BENETTON
Team, now with much improved reliability, still in need of more Ford power. Fabi qualifies miserable tenth after handling problems which also affect Boutsen who starts ninth. Fabi commences race one from pit lane in spare car after wheel bearing problem. Starts race two in repaired race car. Drives non-stop to good fourth place (lapped) despite fuel-shortage misfire. Now seventh equal with Boutsen in

Three points for Fabi but six for 'Jim Clark' Palmer.

Drivers Championship. Boutsen improves to seventh, lap one, and later to fifth. Car jumps out of fourth and fifth gears. Obliged stop eight minutes to cure misfire by changing plugs and engine management box. Finishes dispirited 14th, six laps down.

OSELLA
Caffi qualifies 25th. Retires lap 28 when 17th (turbo). Forini, in second GP, starts 26th. Retires from 16th with rear suspension and wheel-bearing problems, lap 33.

MINARDI
Campos starts race one from 20th on grid and is involved in lap one multiple collision. Starts race two from pit lane and understeers off course, lap 25, when 22nd. Nannini qualifies well at 14th. Races to excellent eighth before dropping to eleventh for second 1987 race finish despite running out of fuel on lap 67.

LIGIER
Megatron engine supply problems overcome by revised financial deal but another miserable race for the unlucky French team. Arnoux starts eighteenth. Destroys car in race one multiple crash. Starts race two in spare. Retires lap 30 when 16th (holed radiator). Ghinzani qualifies 23rd. Retires lap 25 when 15th (ignition).

FERRARI
Continued engine and chassis improvements at last enable team to look fully capable of winning. Berger takes first Ferrari pole position since Brazil 1985. Magnificently leads race from laps two to 67 (except for laps 34/35 when second to Alboreto after tyre stop). With heavily worn tyres spins on lap 68 as result of relentless pressuring by inspired Prost. Finishes second. Alboreto, in spare car after race one collision with Piquet, climbs to second, lap 27, after superb scrap with Piquet and Prost only to retire lap 39 (gearbox). Ferrari delightedly, and to World's acclaim, back in contention after two years of demeaning lack of real success.

LOLA
Alliot again qualifies as fastest 3½ litre driver (19th). Hit by Arnoux Ligier and Danner Zakspeed in race one first lap fracas. Retires spare car lap 32 when 13th (fuel pump failure).

almost become boring to see them at the front. But it was all different now! Lap 27 Alboreto takes Piquet to make it Ferrari first and second — and it was a very long time since we'd seen that.

Then the tyre stops with the inevitable shuffling of places they create. At half distance it was Alboreto in front of Berger, Fabi, Prost, Piquet and De Cesaris — until lap 39 when poor Michele Alboreto, after a superb drive, retired with a recurrence of the gearbox problem that had afflicted him in practice.

But all eyes were now on the incredible Alain Prost. He'd stayed ahead of Piquet after their tyre stops, he'd then caught and passed Fabi who was going through non-stop and now he was second! Not only second but second to car number 28 — Berger's Ferrari — with the knowledge that, coincidentally, if he could get ahead of it he would be on target for the record breaking 28th Grand Prix win that

would make him the most successful World Championship driver of all.

Making it look easy with that deceptively smooth and flowing style of his he went faster and faster — remorselessly closing the gap between his McLaren and the scarlet Ferrari. Lap 41: a new lap record — one minute 20.83 seconds. But Berger responded. First with a lap in one minute 20.02 and then, on lap 66, the fastest of the race in one minute 19.282. But closer and closer drew Prost. From over ten seconds behind to two and a half knowing, he subsequently said, that his only chance of the win he wanted so much was to pressure Berger into making a mistake. And then, on lap 68, with only three to go, it happened — Berger spun and Prost was through into the lead. 'My tyres were shot,' said Gerhard sadly afterwards, 'and Alain was pushing so hard that I just couldn't ease off and I lost it.' He lost it to finish second in a

Derek Warwick didn't hit anything but the earth moved a little.

race which showed, once again, that you can never ignore Alain Prost. In a car restored to full health he'd shown that he was in a class of his own and had hauled himself into a position where he was at least mathematically again in contention for the Championship. Simply superb!

Only Nelson Piquet finished on the same lap as Prost and Berger. His third place was the lowest he'd finished in ten scoring races so far but, now 18 points ahead of Ayrton Senna, he was quietly happy. With the prospect of a third World Championship clearly in view he

had every right to be. But maybe he now needed to be just a little concerned about the indomitable Prost?

As a postscript an acknowledgement of a drive that, in its way, was as good as Prost's. From his pit lane start Jonathan Palmer carved through the field in his 'atmospheric' Tyrrell to finish tenth overall and only one-fifth of a second behind the class-winning Ivan Capelli. A magnificent achievement which consolidated his lead in the 3½ litre Championship and made him, in my view, the joint 'Man of the Day'.

Top man! The most successful of all time.

Yes it is a glamorous life — Michele Alboreto and friends.

PORTUGUESE GRAND PRIX

Winner: Alain Prost, McLaren MP4/3-4   *Fastest Lap:* Gerhard Berger, 122.734 mph

GRID POSITION

No.	Driver
28	Berger
5	Mansell
1	Prost
6	Piquet
12	Senna
27	Alboreto
7	Patrese
2	Johansson
20	Boutsen
19	Fabi
18	Cheever
17	Warwick
8	De Cesaris
24	Nannini
11	Nakajima
10	Danner
9	Brundle
25	Arnoux
30	Alliot
23	Campos
4	Streiff
16	Capelli
26	Ghinzani
3	Palmer
21	Caffi
22	Forini

RESULTS

Pos.	Driver	Car
1	Prost	McLaren-TAG MP4/3-4
2	Berger	Ferrari F187/098
3	Piquet	Williams-Honda FW11B/5
4	Fabi	Benetton-Ford B187-08
5	Johansson	McLaren-Tag MP4/3-5
6	Cheever	Arrows-Megatron A10/3
7	Senna	Lotus-Honda 99T/3
8	Nakajima	Lotus-Honda 99T/3
9	Capelli	March-Cosworth 871/2
10	Palmer	Tyrrell-Cosworth DG/016-6
11	Nannini	Minardi-Moderni M186/3
12	Streiff	Tyrrell-Cosworth DG/016-7
13	Warwick	Arrows-Megatron A10/4
14	Boutsen	Benetton-Ford B187-06

WORLD CHAMPIONSHIP

Drivers	Pts	Constructors	Pts
1. Piquet	67	1. Williams-Honda	110
2. Senna	49	2. McLaren-Tag	62
3. Mansell	43	3. Lotus-Honda	55
4. Prost	40	4. Ferrari	26
5. Johansson	22	5. Benetton-Ford	20
6. Berger	18	6. Arrows-Megatron	8
7. Boutsen	10	7. Tyrrell-Cosworth	8
Fabi	10	8. Brabham-BMW	6
9. Alboreto	8	9. Zakspeed	2
10. Nakajima	6	10. Ligier-Megatron	1
11. Cheever	5	Lola-Cosworth	1
12. De Cesaris	4	March-Cosworth	1
Palmer	4		
Streiff	4		
15. Warwick	3		
16. Brundle	2		
Patrese	2		
18. Alliot	1		
Arnoux	1		
Capelli	1		

JIM CLARK CUP		COLIN CHAPMAN CUP	
1. Palmer	71	1. Tyrrell-Cosworth	129
2. Streiff	58	2. AGS-Cosworth	35
3. Fabre	35	3. March-Cosworth	34
4. Capelli	34	4. Lola-Cosworth	25
5. Alliot	25		

27th September 1987
Circuit: Jerez

NO sooner was the Portuguese Grand Prix over than it was time to go to Spain for Round 13 of the World Championship — the last in Europe — just one week later. From the most westerly point in Europe to almost the most southerly — the Sherry city of Jerez near the Gulf of Cadiz and not far from Gibraltar. As we motored there through the glorious Spanish mountain scenery with its forests of chestnut and cork trees, excitedly recalling the great race we'd just seen, little did we know that we were soon to witness another which would put even Portugal in the shade! In very different ways the two men who had finished first and second at Jerez the year before separated by a razor-thin 14/1,000th of a second; Ayrton Senna and Nigel Mansell, were again to make the pace — hotly challenged by no less than six of Grand Prix racing's other top men in another truly memorable race.

Jerez is a brand new circuit specially built to replace the unloved track at Jarama near Madrid. 2.6 miles long it writhes around the floor of a rocky valley, has absolutely superb facilities and is liked by the drivers — but not, it strangely seems, by the Spanish. In 1986, its first year which produced a magnificent race, there seemed to be more people in the paddock than there were in the many excellent grandstands. 1987 wasn't all that much better. They missed a lot!

Senna — the head of the 'snake' in oily Camel Lotus, chased by Boutsen.

In comparison with Portugal Jerez is a 'slow' circuit. Sixteen corners including an S bend, two second-gear hairpins and only one real, short, straight make it very difficult for the drivers to generate a smooth-flowing racing rhythm and its comparatively low speed closes

the performance gap between the turbo and atmospheric cars — as we were to see.

In two days of high-key excitement the practice was almost as dramatic as the race which was to follow, as Mansell, Piquet, Berger and Alboreto battled for grid supremacy. Thanks to all the hard work done by Dr Harvey Postlethwaite on the Ferrari aerodynamics and suspension set-up, allied to the better spread of power that the Maranello engine men had achieved, the scarlet 187s were again right on the pace at Jerez and were looking for their second successive pole position. With an 'Active' and a 'Passive' suspension car each Mansell and Piquet could take their pick from whichever suited the circuit best — and as far as Nigel was concerned it was his 'Passive' car. With just over fifteen minutes of practice to go he was secure in his eighth pole position of the year — until Piquet, in his now usual 'Active' car, went out on his second set of qualifiers! And when he did so it was clear that he had been hiding his hand from his team-mate all along for he flew round in one minute 22.46 seconds (115.090 mph) — almost ⁶⁄₁₀ of a second faster than Mansell's best. And that's a lot!

Out on the circuit in his 'Passive' car Mansell got the news by radio. Furiously realising that he'd been duped he shot into the pit lane to change cars in the dying minutes of practice only to be faced with the red light which told him to stop as he'd been randomly selected to have his car weighed. Out of it jumped Nigel to run down the pit lane and get into his 'Active' car — and for breaking the regulations he was fined US$3,000 and had his Saturday times disallowed. Not that that mattered — his Friday time had been faster. But it was a very angry Nigel Mansell who faced the prospect of 'only' starting second on the grid the next day (his 14th successive front row start — a superb achievement).

Behind him, on row two, would be the Ferraris of Berger and Alboreto followed by Senna (troubled by lack of grip), Fabi (Benet-

Campos spins again — this time on lap 1 of his home G.P. — he finished last.

ton), a disappointed Alain Prost (McLaren) in a lowly seventh place due to a recurrence of the TAG engine misfire problem, and Thierry Boutsen (Benetton). So with both Williams, both Ferraris, both Benettons, a McLaren and a Lotus in the top eight things looked good! After Sunday's more realistic half-hour of final practice they looked even better for Berger was fastest with Alliot's Lola, the fastest 3½ litre car, less than three seconds off the pace in race trim.

What was to be the most absorbing race of the season so far was decided at the end of the first lap when Nigel Mansell, from second on the grid, thrust past Piquet into a lead he was never to lose for the whole 72 laps — including his tyre stop. I've seen a lot of Grands Prix in my time but never have I seen a

more awesome and dominating display of skill and determination than that of Mansell at Jerez on the day he kept alive his hopes of winning the 1987 World Championship by winning his fifth race of the year.

With Piquet second it was Senna who set the pattern of the race for 62 of its 72 laps. With a low-downforce set-up to give him speed on the straights at the expense of speed in the corners, and with the intention of going through the race non-stop (as he had done so successfully the year before) he blasted past Alboreto and Berger and into third place as the lights turned to green.

Piquet second. Senna third. Berger fourth. Alboreto fifth. Boutsen sixth and Fabi seventh. And that's the way it stayed for 28 laps (except that Alboreto passed Berger on lap 13). Sounds dull. It was anything but! The six-car, brightly coloured, blaring, weaving, 5,000 horsepower 'snake' blasting round Jerez was a brilliant display of Grand Prix racing at its riveting best and made you realise why today's GP drivers richly deserve their mammoth incomes.

Lap 27 and Alain Prost, driving with his head as well as his heart — as usual — made the first tyre stop of the leaders. After passing the rapid-starting Andrea De Cesaris to take eighth place behind Fabi on lap seven Alain had inched his way up to the tail of the 'snake'. Coolly working it out as he lapped at some 110 mph he figured it would pay to get the new rubber on early and then pick off the leaders as their grip diminished. Which is precisely what he did. After an 11.34 seconds stop he rejoined just one place down — ninth behind Johansson. On lap 29 he was past Fabi to eighth. Lap 32 seventh (Boutsen in for tyres). Lap 35 in the points at sixth (Johansson in).

At half distance, lap 36, Mansell, benefiting from a clear track and with his rivals denying each other the best racing line as they squabbled for places, had a lead of 24 seconds. After he'd made his 11.35 seconds stop on lap 43 he rejoined the track still in the lead a car's length ahead of Piquet who, try as he may — and he did! — couldn't get past his inspired team-mate.

But now Prost, sixth, and the fastest man at Jerez, was right up with the three car battle for third — Senna, Alboreto and Berger. On lap

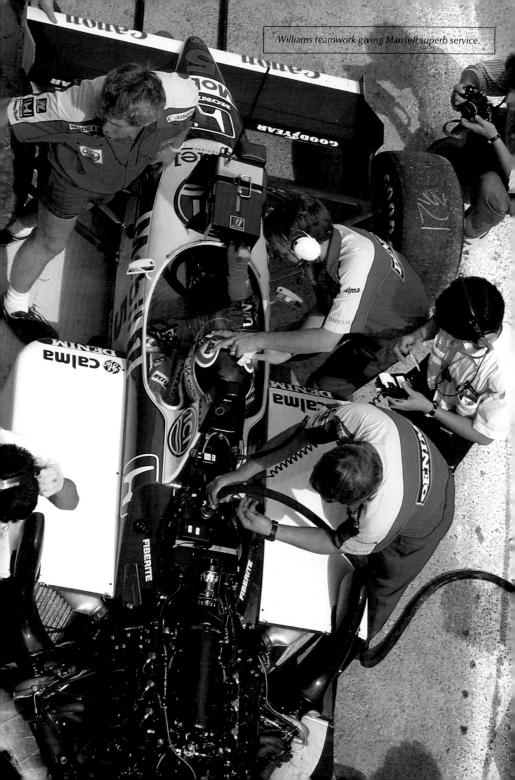

Team Analysis

McLAREN

Good race for McLaren albeit with overtones of concern due to return of TAG engine misfire problem. After superb Portugal win Prost qualifies disappointed seventh. Initially drops to ninth but recovers to seventh laps 7 to 26. Opts for tactical early tyre stop (lap 27). Fourth by lap 44. To third as Piquet spins lap 46 and finishes second after Piquet again goes off lap 67. Remains fourth in Championship with third successive victory still possible as, unlike leader Piquet, can count all points from remaining three races. Johansson starts eleventh. After steady progress despite low-downforce understeer finishes excellent third. Team now second in Constructors Championship but impossible to catch Williams.

Johansson was donated 3rd place after Piquet's late pit stop.

TYRRELL

'Slow' Jerez circuit suits 'Atmospheric' Tyrrell team. Palmer starts 16th (second non-turbo). Gains six places lap one. Leads 3½ litre class in close combat with Alliot. Improved to excellent ninth by lap 41. Outrageously pushed off by Arnoux lap 56 when still ninth and on target for sixth class win. Still leads 'Atmospheric' Championship. Streiff qualifies 15th and top 3½ litre. Drives steady and strong race to finish seventh (second in class). Now only seven points behind Palmer in Class Championship.

WILLIAMS

Riccardo Patrese officially announced as Piquet replacement for 1988. Team again provides both Piquet and Mansell with 'Active' and 'Passive' cars. Piquet audaciously takes fourth pole position of '87 in 'Active' car in closing stages of final practice after hoodwinking Mansell. Mansell fined US$3,000 by FISA for Saturday failure to comply with car weighing rules. From second on grid in 'Passive' car (14th successive front row start) Mansell takes lead at end of first lap and totally dominates race to take fifth 1987 win and move ahead of Senna to second in Championship. Slim chance of Championship victory improved — all points from remaining three races will count. Piquet second laps 1 to 45. Disastrous

19 second tyre stop (driver's fault). Spins lap 48 when fourth. Regains second lap 63 but goes off lap 67 necessitating precautionary pit stop. Finishes fourth. Leads Mansell by 18 points in Championship but, now with eleven scores, must discard points if scores again.

BRABHAM

Both drivers on row five of starting grid. Patrese ninth. De Cesaris tenth. Patrese runs 12th laps 4-15 but then, beset by grip problems, slides to back of field with four stops for tyres. Finishes 13th, four laps down. After initial improvement to eighth De Cesaris retains starting place until lap 27 when retires with broken gearbox.

ZAKSPEED

Brundle qualifies 20th after engine problems. Gradually improves to finish exhausted in 11th place, two laps down, after wrestling with overweight car. Danner starts 22nd. To pits lap 12 when 21st for new engine management box. Retires from 20th and last, lap 51 (gearbox).

LOTUS

Senna, 1986 winner by 14/1000 of second ahead of Mansell, qualifies fifth. Sprints to third at first corner. In low downforce car is quick on straights but slow through corners. In non-stop race doggedly holds third place, and then second, creating frustrated crocodile of top men behind him, until lap 63 when has to give way with worn-out tyres. Finishes fifth and drops to third in Championship — but still a potential winner. Nakajima starts first Jerez race 18th. Spins lap 16 but improves in non-stop run to finish 9th (two laps down). Team now third in Constructors Championship 15 points behind McLaren.

AGS

Roberto Moreno test session at Paul Ricard dramatically improves car set-up. Fabre qualifies 25th ahead of both turbo Osellas. Retires lap 11 (clutch hydraulics) when 25th and last.

Palmer leading Alliot (with Mansell looming). This superb scrap was ruined by Arnoux when he rammed the Englishman.

Nelson made 'more mistakes than in the whole of the rest of the season'. He still finished 4th.

MARCH

Poor practice sees Capelli qualify 19th. Despite four spins and grass in sidepods finishes 12th (third in class).

ARROWS

Expensive practice for team with multiple Megatron engine failures (some due to drivers). Warwick qualifies 12th, collides with dreaded Arnoux lap one and pits for new nosecone. Recovers well to finish 10th (two laps down). Cheever starts 13th and finishes good eighth in car vastly improved after lap 21 tyre stop. Team relieved to finish both cars after troubled practice.

BENETTON

Fabi sixth and Boutsen eighth on grid. Boutsen drives superb race as part of Senna-led 'snake'. Sixth laps one to 31. After lap 32 tyre stop passes Alboreto and Prost to third lap 55. Pressurises Senna for second laps 55-59. Retires from briefly held second place lap 67 when brakes fail causing retirement spin into sand trap. Fabi races seventh at tail of 'snake' laps 1-29. Retires from 9th, lap 41, after tyre stop (engine). Team retain Constructors Championship fifth place.

OSELLA

Both Caffi and Forini fail to qualify.

MINARDI

Campos lacklustre at home GP. Qualifies 24th after damaging car in off-course spin. Spins to tail of field lap one. Drives round at back to finish 14th (four laps down). Nannini starts from 21st Briskly climbs to 16th lap two. Retires from 15th lap 45 (turbo).

LIGIER

Arnoux starts from 14th with new chassis after Portuguese GP lap one destruction derby. Collides with Warwick lap one and rams Palmer when being lapped (lap 56). Retires lap 56 (engine). Ghinzani 23rd on grid. Retires from 21st lap 25 (ignition pick up).

FERRARI

Hard work by Harvey Postlethwaite on aerodynamics and suspension set-up, in association with greatly improved engine power-spread, enables Berger (third) and Alboreto (fourth) to occupy row two of grid (despite Alboreto Saturday crash). Both men excellent in race running fourth and fifth in Senna-led 'snake' for 43 laps. After late pit stops (Berger lap 47: Alboreto lap 52) Berger retires from sixth, lap 63 (engine), and Alboreto from fourth, lap 68 (engine). Berger creates lap record.

LOLA

At circuit which suits 'Atmospheric' cars superb race for likeable and enthusiastic, Gerard Larrousse-led, French team. After qualifying 17th (third in class) Alliot battles with Palmer for class leadership. Takes ninth place lap 56 when Palmer punted off by Arnoux. Benefits from Boutsen, Berger and Alboreto retirements to take second overall sixth place of season (only one lap down), win 3½ litre class for third time and take second 1987 World Championship point.

COLONI

Nicola Larini in new Italian car which failed to qualify at Monza, starts 26th in first GP for car and driver. Retires lap nine when 22nd (left rear suspension breakage).

Germany's Grand Prix driver Christian Danner couldn't get into gear.

44, with an inspired piece of opportunistic driving the Frenchman took both the Ferraris on the inside of the Pits Hairpin. Sixth to fourth in one surgical move!

Lap 46 and Piquet starts an uncharacteristic run of mistakes which resulted in his lowest Grand Prix finish of 1987. Into the pits for new tyres in second place. Out of them after an abysmal stop of 19 seconds in fourth place behind Mansell, Senna and Prost and only ahead of Berger because he nearly took the nose of the Ferrari as he sliced back on to the racing line (which it doesn't pay to leave at Jerez as he was later to confirm). 19 seconds? Yes because Nelson hadn't got his foot on the brake pedal and his tyre men couldn't get the new rear wheels on to the spinning hubs!

Nelson fought back. But too hard. For as he left the racing line on lap 48 to take third from Prost he instantly spun on the 'marbles'. Down to sixth as Alboreto and Boutsen shot past. Meantime Berger, who had pitted on lap 47, was really flying on new grippy Goodyears. A new lap record on lap 49 (one minute 26.986 seconds = 108.47 mph — the fastest of the race) brought him back into contention but now all eyes were on Thierry Boutsen as the quiet and charming Belgian made his bid.

To fourth on lap 52 as Alboreto pitted. And then to third, past Prost and Piquet, there to harry Senna unmercifully for lap after lap — nearly sawing the Lotus gearbox in half with his Benetton nosecone. Remember Senna? He was still brilliantly there on his non-stop run, in second place since lap 46, exploiting his 'low downforce' speed to pull away on the

The brilliance of Alain Prost — as the Ferraris fought each other he whipped by.

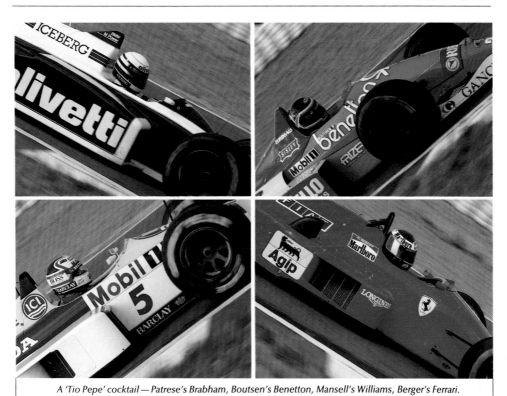

A 'Tio Pepe' cocktail — Patrese's Brabham, Boutsen's Benetton, Mansell's Williams, Berger's Ferrari.

straights and grimly sticking to the racing line as his rivals, with greater grip, piled up behind him on the corners. But on lap 63 an almost gripless Ayrton, with Piquet now third, Boutsen down to fourth (failing brakes) and a smoking Berger Ferrari about to expire, had to give way. Down to fifth as Piquet, Boutsen and Prost raced past him.

But even now the pattern of the Spanish Grand Prix was to alter dramatically — on lap 67 with five to go — Piquet went off, but within 50 yards, Boutsen having taken the Brazilian's second place, shot into a sand trap as his brakes finally gave up, letting the fast recovering Piquet back into second! So Nelson had it made. His seventh second place of 1987 which would surely clinch his third World Championship? But no! Everybody's danger man Alain Prost was there — past Nelson to second. And there to stay.

In a race where 'I made more mistakes than I have in the whole of the rest of the season'

Piquet made another precautionary pit stop and that let Johansson through into third for the jinx-ridden Alboreto, after a superb race, had retired with a blown engine two laps earlier. But in a situation where it had been impossible to take your eyes away from the thrilling battle at the front far too few people realised that once again Jonathan Palmer, in his 3½ litre Tyrrell, was having a blinder of a race — in very close company indeed with Philippe Alliot's Lola. Until a typically boorish Rene Arnoux move on lap 56 pushed Palmer, now ninth, off the course and out of the race — to deny him his sixth class win of the season. But Jonathan's loss was Philip's gain for the Frenchman not only won the 'atmospheric' race but finished sixth overall, only one lap behind Mansell, to score his second 1987 World Championship point — an excellent achievement.

So Nigel Mansell brilliantly won his fifth Grand Prix of 1987, revenged himself on Senna

115

for his 1986 defeat, showed that his faith in the 'passive' Williams was fully justified, once again beat Piquet fair and square and climbed the podium with a still slim, but improved, chance of winning the 1987 World Championship. 'After Adelaide last year Murray did you think I'd give up?'

And now the gruelling prospect of three long-haul races in four weeks. Mexico 18th October. Japan 1st November. Australia 15th November. with Piquet, Mansell, Senna and Prost all still capable of ending the year as Number One. Something to savour!

The crowd thought it was great — all seven of them.

Viva La Differencia!

SPANISH GRAND PRIX

Winner: Nigel Mansell, Williams FW11B/3   *Fastest Lap:* Gerhard Berger, 108.489 mph

GRID POSITION		RESULTS			WORLD CHAMPIONSHIP				
No.	Driver	Pos.	Driver	Car	Drivers	Pts	Constructors		Pts
	6 Piquet	1	Mansell	Williams-Honda FW11B/3	1. Piquet	70	1.	Williams-Honda	122
5	Mansell	2	Prost	McLaren-TAG MP4/3-4	2. Mansell	52	2.	McLaren-TAG	72
28	Berger	3	Johansson	McLaren-TAG MP4/3-5	3. Senna	51	3.	Lotus-Honda	57
27	Alboreto	4	Piquet	Williams-Honda FW11B/5	4. Prost	46	4.	Ferrari	26
12	Senna	5	Senna	Lotus-Honda 99T/4	5. Johansson	26	5.	Benetton-Ford	20
19	Fabi	6	Alliot	Lola-Cosworth LC87/02	6. Berger	18	6.	Arrows-Megatron	8
1	Prost	7	Streiff	Tyrrell-Cosworth DG/016-3	7. Boutsen	10		Tyrrell-Cosworth	8
20	Boutsen	8	Cheever	Arrows-Megatron A10/2	Fabi	10	8.	Brabham-BMW	6
7	Patrese	9	Nakajima	Lotus-Honda 99T/3	9. Alboreto	8	9.	Lola-Cosworth	2
8	De Cesaris	10	Warwick	Arrows-Megatron A10/4	10. Nakajima	6		Zakspeed	2
2	Johansson	11	Brundle	Zakspeed 871/03	11. Cheever	5	11.	Ligier-Megatron	1
17	Warwick	12	Capelli	March-Cosworth 871/2	12. De Cesaris	4		March-Cosworth	1
18	Cheever	13	Patrese	Brabham-BMW BT56/4	Palmer	4			
25	Arnoux	14	Campos	Minardi-Moderni M186/1	Streiff	4			
4	Streiff				15. Warwick	3			
3	Palmer				16. Alliot	2			
30	Alliot				Brundle	2			
11	Nakajima				Patrese	2			
16	Capelli				19. Arnoux	1			
9	Brundle				Capelli	1			
24	Nannini								
10	Danner				**JIM CLARK CUP**		**COLIN CHAPMAN CUP**		
26	Ghinzani				1. Palmer	71	1.	Tyrrell-Cosworth	135
23	Campos				2. Streiff	64	2.	March-Cosworth	38
14	Fabre				3. Capelli	38	3.	AGS-Cosworth	35
32	Larini				4. Fabre	35	4.	Lola-Cosworth	34
					5. Alliot	34			

MEXICO

18th October 1987
Circuit: Autodromo Hermanos Rodriguez

THE Mexican Grand Prix was like the Curate's egg — good in parts. But the good parts were sensational and at the end of it only two men were left in the running for motor racing's greatest prize — those 'jolly chums' Nelson Piquet and Nigel Mansell. But was the all-important gap between them nine points or twelve? That depended on whether Piquet would be disqualified for receiving a lap one push-start after he'd spun to a standstill and stalled his engine. In the end the speculation that he would be, and that Mansell's championship chances would be improved thereby, turned out to be groundless. Under the circumstances it would have been a travesty of justice to exclude Nelson but in spite of his seventh second-place of 1987 a sixth Mansell victory meant that Nigel might still be able to carry the prestigious Number One on his Williams in 1988.

Mexico is a returnee to the World Championship scene having been re-instated to the calendar in 1986 after a sixteen year gap triggered by non-existent control of massive course-invading crowds. The race location was as before — on the outskirts of Mexico City — the excellent 2.7 mile Hermanos Rodriguez circuit (posthumously named after the country's two Grand Prix heroes the Rodriguez brothers Pedro and Riccardo) which had been impressively updated at vast expense.

The 1987 facilities were even better but there was universal condemnation of the track's appalling bumpiness — criticism which was vehemently dismissed by FISA President Jean-Marie Ballestre combined with an illogical announcement that he intended to ban 'Active'-suspension in 1988! But whilst the circuit layout was challengingly good a lot of other things weren't. The notorious Mexico City smog. The endless traffic jams. The local police who augmented their incomes with hefty on-the-spot fines (no receipt!) for imaginary traffic offences. The earthquake-ravaged buildings and the resultant thousands of miserably deprived people existing in windowless corrugated iron shanties. The ravening guard dogs — no respectors of the 'Free Access' FISA pass. And the seemingly inevitable result of the heat, the height and the local food — the Aztec Two-Step, Monte-

'Banzai' Nakajima on his last lap — it was also his first. Seconds later he rammed Warwick — Johansson and Danner (seen here) hit each other avoiding the Lotus.

zuma's Revenge or the Mexican Trots. Call it what you will the unpleasant results are the same!

1986 established two other unique characteristics of the circuit. Its power-sapping altitude — at 7,000 feet the air is thin — and its voracious appetite for tyres. The height was no problem for the turbo teams — they just

No improvement for Capelli in the Jim Clark trophy contest — despite excellent practice he retired from the race.

was the structural strength of their cars' carbon-fibre tubs which saved them from serious injury — another tribute to modern design, materials and construction.

With only $^6/_{10}$ of a second covering the top six qualifiers Nigel Mansell took his eighth pole of the season ahead of Berger, Piquet (in a 'passive' Williams as was Mansell), Boutsen, Prost and Fabi. With a Ferrari and the two Benettons all within a whisker of Nigel's pole time it was going to be close at the front. But would Prost, still a Championship 'possible', and Johansson last the distance after a stream of different TAG engine problems with their McLarens? We'd see!

One of the good things about Mexico is the weather and race day was no exception for it could not have been better. Temperature hot. Humidity nil and sky clear. Last year in similar conditions the tyres had taken a terrible beating with some drivers stopping three times for new rubber. It would be different this year though as Goodyear, benefiting both from their 1987 experiences and their 'lesson' from '86 (when Berger won thanks to a non-stop run on Pirellis), made an exception to their previously rigid 'one compound' rule. They had brought two alternatives, supplying the teams with their usual 'Cs' and a harder 'B' compound which only Piquet chose to use in the race.

turned up the boost to compensate. But for the 'Atmospheric' runners whose Cosworths were gasping for oxygen the result was a power deficiency of some 450 horsepower which made them fear that they'd be lucky to do the mandatory 90% of race-distance required to earn Championship points. How gloriously wrong they were!

Friday and Saturday's practice sessions were notable for four things — Nigel Mansell and Ayrton Senna were lucky to finish them alive. Ferrari and Benetton again looked like being real competition for the dominant Williams duo. McLaren had got it all wrong with their TAG engines. And the track was dangerously bumpy.

Both Mansell and Senna lost control of their cars exiting the 165 mph banked Pits Bend which leads on to the circuit's longest straight — and Warwick was to do the same in the race. Mansell had scrubbed off most of his speed by the time he hit the pit wall backwards but Senna slammed sideways into the tyre-cushioned barrier at some 130 mph. It

After the preliminaries the Mexican Grand Prix began with the usual spectacular blast down to the first corner followed, seconds later, by an incident which led to the removal of Alain Prost from both the race and the World Championship. Who caused it depends on who you are talking to but, in trying to pass Piquet to take third place, Prost collided with the Williams, bent his steering-arm and spun Nelson to a standstill with a stalled engine. The start of a walk back to the pits for Alain and one of the most scintillating drives of the year for Nelson as, after a push start that was to cause speculation and confusion, he stormed back into action.

Meantime, back at the front, Berger and Boutsen had broken away to start an enthralling battle for the lead pursued by a slow-starting Nigel Mansell, followed by Michele Alboreto, Teo Fabi, Ayrton Senna and the two Brabhams of Patrese and De Cesaris. Ferrari first and Benetton second! Was Mexico going

*Leading a Grand Prix for the first time — the 'charming' Thierry Boutsen —
electrical failure cheated him of victory.*

to see the breaking of the Williams' stranglehold?

No time to think about that now — look at the TV — Nakajima's gone mad! It wasn't a case of the Japanese braking late — he didn't seem to have braked at all as, to the startled amazement of millions of worldwide viewers, he drove straight into the back of Derek Warwick's Arrows to remove, with clinical precision, his right front wheel and himself from the race. And whilst Derek stumbled back to the pits for a new rear wing and undertray Stefan Johansson and Christian Danner drove into each other trying to avoid Nakajima. Piquet down to last and four out on the first lap — including both McLarens!

But now, on lap two, something new in Grand Prix racing. Boutsen leads! The quiet

Also a part-time leader — Gerhard Berger — a broken turbo stopped his winning drive.

Team Analysis

McLAREN

McLaren's worst Grand Prix since Monaco 1983 (when both Lauda and Watson failed even to qualify). Mexico altitude causes multiple TAG engine blow-ups affecting both drivers — who qualify fifth (Prost) and fifteenth (Johansson). Prost makes rare mistake on first lap and collides with Piquet causing immediate retirement (bent steering arm) and total destruction of World Championship hopes. Johansson collides into retirement with Danner as both try to avoid Nakajima's three-wheeled Lotus on lap two.

TYRRELL

Amazingly good race for Tyrrell in view of major power loss for 'Atmospheric' Cosworth engines caused by 7,000 foot Mexico altitude (some 450 horsepower down on turbos). Palmer qualifies 22nd following misfire and incorrect tyre choice. Nevertheless finishes excellent seventh (and second in class) three laps down to extend Jim Clark Trophy lead over Streiff to nine points. Streiff starts 25th (oil pump problems) and finishes praiseworthy eighth (three laps down) after steady and reliable race.

WILLIAMS

Dramatic and significant meeting for team with both drivers in normally-suspended cars. After miraculous escape from 160 mph course-departure on Friday Mansell superbly takes eighth pole position of season (and fifteenth consecutive grid front-row — a record). After leading race in rebuilt car until lap 32 stoppage cannily races second to Piquet after restart

calmly to win his sixth GP of 1987 by 26 seconds on aggregate of times. Piquet, third on grid, starts in hastily repaired car after Sunday warm-up assault by inevitable Arnoux. Then nudged into lap one spin by Prost. After push start by marshals brilliantly drives from last to fourth before lap 32 race stoppage. Finishes first in restarted race with record lap at 124.97 mph to take second place overall on aggregate of times. Championship gap between leader Piquet and Mansell, one of whom must win, now twelve points.

A disastrous meeting for McLaren — both cars were out in the first lap.

BRABHAM

Excellent race for team showing continued improvement. Patrese qualifies eighth and finishes delighted third — his first podium position since 1984. De Cesaris starts tenth and drives excellent race contesting second place with Senna until 'pushed off' (lap 23).

ZAKSPEED

Brundle optimistic for good race as a result of performance improvement following re-mapped engine electronics. Starts 13th with non-stop intentions but stops nevertheless — to retire on lap four (turbo). Danner qualifies 17th. Tangles with Johansson, lap two, trying to avoid Nakajima's wheel-off Lotus, and retires. Awful race for the team.

LOTUS

A race to forget! Nakajima (first time at Mexico) qualifies 16th and then rams Warwick Arrows, lap one, neatly removing right front wheel from Lotus and himself from race. Senna departs Pits Bend, Friday, at 160 mph. Unhurt but severely shaken. Qualifies seventh. Starts in rebuilt accident car. Running increasingly distant second with failing clutch when race stopped. Clutch gives up after restart causing missed gear, spin and stalled engine (lap 55). Senna, furious with marshals' refusal to push-start him, exits car, World Championship chances destroyed, clouts official and is fined $15,000 for doing so.

A very fine third place for Riccardo Patrese who deservedly got back on to the podium after three unrewarding years.

AGS

Pascal Fabre fails to qualify.

MARCH

Good practice for Capelli who qualifies 20th as fastest 'Atmospheric' driver, six seconds off pace. Leads class until spin caused by cracked engine-bearer. After pit lane late start following bearer replacement races last until lap 52 retirement (engine).

ARROWS

Another mixed but encouraging race. On 'impossibly bumpy' circuit which seems to affect Arrows more than most' Derek Warwick qualifies eleventh. After being rammed by Nakajima, lap one, loses three laps replacing rear wing and undertray. Causes race stoppage, lap 32, by going off at 160 mph Pits Bend, probably due to Nakajima-induced component breakage. Two wheels off car. Shaken but, amazingly, unhurt. Unsurprisingly does not restart. Cheever, in 100th GP, starts twelfth and drives full distance to excellent fourth place. Arrows move up to sixth in Constructors' Championship.

BENETTON

Benetton lead for the first time in 1987! After qualifying fourth and being fastest in Sunday warm-up Boutsen impressively leads lap two to fourteen only to retire (lap 15: electronics) when calmly confident of victory. Fabi, sixth on grid, finishes sixth (two laps down) after two stops — one to clear radiators of grass (spin) and the other for tyres. Team now only four points behind fourth-placed Ferrari in Constructors' Championship.

OSELLA

Caffi qualifies 26th and last in new-livery car. Retires lap 51 (engine).

MINARDI

Campos 19th on grid. Running 15th and last with misfire and gear-linkage problem when race stopped. Fails to restart. Nannini qualifies well at 14th. Having run an excellent ninth for thirteen laps retires lap 14 with usual Minardi problem — broken Motori Moderni engine.

LIGIER

Arnoux qualifies 18th. After hitting Piquet in Sunday warm-up obliged to start in spare car. Retires lap 30 (ignition). Ghinzani 21st on grid. Running eighth (lapped) when race stopped. Retires lap 44 (engine). Team, desperate to reach Constructors' Championship Top Ten to benefit from FOCA end of season awards structure, still eleventh with only one point.

FERRARI

With continued unreliability frustration for Berger, misery for Alboreto and gloom for team. 1986 winner Berger (in Benetton-BMW) qualifies superb second only 4/100ths of a second behind Mansell. Using spare car ('handles better') leads lap one and runs challenging second to Boutsen laps 2-14 before retiring lap 21 (turbo) whilst leading. Alboreto, a delighted father since Spanish GP, troubled by handling, engine and traffic, starts ninth. Improves to sixth but retires for eleventh time in 1987 (lap 13: engine). With 20 retirements from 28 starts team only has 26 Constructors' Championship points.

LOLA

First two-car race for Camels-Lola team. Second car most impressively driven by 26-year-old Formula Renault/Formula Three/Formula 3000 ace, Frenchman Yannick Dalmas who out-qualifies Alliot to 23rd on grid (third 3½ litre) and finishes excellent ninth (four laps down) in first GP. After qualifying 24th Alliot again drives fine race to finish sixth overall, win class, take a World Championship point and advance two places to third in Jim Clark 'Atmospheric' Drivers' Championship. Team naturally delighted with two high-place finishes.

A superb first Grand Prix for Yannick Dalmas who out-qualified team-mate Alliot and finished ninth.

and charming Belgian was at last where he'd threatened to be for a long time — and where he richly deserved to be — in front in his Benetton-Ford. And looking and feeling totally confident in a car which was handling beautifully and clearly had the power. Two laps later with Boutsen leading Berger (who had himself led on the first lap), Mansell, Senna, Alboreto, De Cesaris (up from tenth on the grid), Fabi, Patrese and a hard-charging Nannini went Martin Brundle with a broken turbo. So, with both cars out, it had already been as bad a day for Zakspeed as it has been for McLaren.

On the fifteenth lap Boutsen's and Benetton's hopes were dashed as Berger, who had been swarming round the Belgian's gearbox, moved back into the lead and Thierry drove sadly into the pit lane to retire with electrical failure. For thirteen laps he had coolly and impressively led a Grand Prix for the first time and was confident that he could have won. His time will come. So were we to see a Ferrari win instead? Not here. For just seven laps later; the twenty-first, a telling plume of solid white smoke from the back of Berger's car showed that his race too was over as he joined his team-mate Michele Alboreto whose engine had given up on the thirteenth lap. Once again both Ferraris had failed to finish.

Lap 21. Enter Williams! Nigel Mansell leads Ayrton Senna with De Cesaris an excellent third right up with the Lotus ahead of Patrese, Cheever and Piquet. Piquet? Yes Piquet! For Nelson, driving at ten-tenths and putting up a succession of fastest laps as people speculated about whether he would be disqualified for his push-start, had scythed his way past twenty of his rivals since he'd dropped to last on lap one.

And as De Cesaris angrily departed the scene on lap 23 ('Senna pushed me off as I tried to pass him when he missed a gear') Piquet took Cheever to move to an incredible fourth place — undoubtedly the man of the race so far. And his decision to start on those harder Goodyear 'Bs' might even enable him to close the 45 second gap between himself and race leader Mansell in the remaining forty laps.

But there weren't forty laps left! With Mansell securely ahead, Senna second and Patrese racing an inspired third only four

seconds behind the Lotus, Derek Warwick shot off the course at some 160 mph and straight into the tyre wall at the notorious Pits Bend. It was a miracle that he wasn't at least badly injured but, mercifully, after what seemed like an age as he sat stunned and motionless in the Arrows, he got out unharmed.

Out came the black and red flags on lap 31 to stop the race whilst the broken Arrows was craned away from its dangerous position. With less than half the distance completed the Mexican Grand Prix would be restarted for a new total distance of 63 laps and the final positions would be based on an aggregate of the two sets of times — the first time that this had happened since the 1984 British Grand Prix at Brands Hatch.

Fifteen drivers restarted for the 33 lap 'second heat' (all on new tyres — to Piquet's understandable displeasure!) and Nelson showed that he meant business right from the off. Straight into the lead despite two strenuous efforts by Mansell to take him and past Patrese into third place on aggregate on lap 33. By lap 38 he was second overall and cutting into Mansell's commanding lead as the Englishman methodically watched his pace knowing that his lead on aggregate was secure provided he made no mistakes. But then, on lap 55, came the sensational incident which lost Senna third place, terminated his race, cost him a lot of money and, much worse, destroyed his slim remaining chance of winning the Championship.

Ayrton's clutch had been failing in the first 'heat'. It was worked on in the between-races interval but after the second start it gave up. Making a clutchless change Senna missed a gear, spun and stalled. Frantically he gestured the marshals to push-start him away from what, following the Piquet precedent, would certainly have been adjudged to have been a 'dangerous position' (and therefore have incurred no penalty). But they did no more than gently trundle him along with one of them endeavouring to get Senna to steer the Lotus off the course. Finally Senna furiously got out of the car, thumped an official and strode off in an almost visible red mist to incur a fine of $15,000 for his conduct.

So Nigel Mansell won his sixth Grand Prix of 1987 to keep his Championship hopes alive.

Nigel had it all in Mexico — a miraculously unscathed practice crash — his eighth 'pole position' of '87 — a canny race to his 13th Grand Prix win, and plaudits (!?) from sponsor ICI's Mike Francis.

Man of the race! In 38 glorious laps Nelson Piquet drove from last to second and stayed there.

High-speed track cleaners — Mexican style.

Second with a superb record lap in one minute 19.13 seconds (124.98 mph) and unpenalised for his lap one push-start was Piquet. Patrese was a delighted third ahead of Cheever and Fabi whilst a magnificent sixth, seventh, eighth and ninth were the 3½ litre cars of Alliot, Palmer, Streiff and newcomer Yannick Dalmas — in a race where, when it began, they had thought that they'd be lucky to do the 90% of the distance they needed to score Championship points!

Maybe not the most exciting of Grands Prix but one full of interest and incident and which — to everyone's immense relief (except Piquet's!) — had failed to resolve the Drivers' Championship. So now would Honda 'let' Mansell do well in Japan? Two weeks later we would know!

MEXICAN GRAND PRIX

Winner: Nigel Mansell, Williams FW11B/1   *Fastest Lap:* Nelson Piquet, 124.980 mph

GRID POSITION		RESULTS			WORLD CHAMPIONSHIP				
No.	Driver	Pos.	Driver	Car	Drivers		Pts	Constructors	Pts
	5 Mansell	1	Mansell	Williams-Honda FW11B/1	1.	Piquet	73	1. Williams-Honda	137
28	Berger	2	Piquet	Williams-Honda FW11B/4	2.	Mansell	61	2. McLaren-TAG	72
6	Piquet	3	Patrese	Brabham-BMW BT56/4	3.	Senna	51	3. Lotus-Honda	57
20	Boutsen	4	Cheever	Arrows-Megatron A10/2	4.	Prost	46	4. Ferrari	26
1	Prost	5	Fabi	Benetton-Ford B187-08	5.	Johansson	26	5. Benetton-Ford	22
19	Fabi	6	Alliot	Lola-Cosworth LC87/03	6.	Berger	18	6. Arrows-Megatron	11
12	Senna	7	Palmer	Tyrrell-Cosworth DG/016-5	7.	Fabi	12	7. Brabham-BMW	10
7	Patrese	8	Streiff	Tyrrell-Cosworth DG/016-2	8.	Boutsen	10	8. Tyrrell-Cosworth	8
27	Alboreto	9	Dalmas	Lola-Cosworth LC87/02	9.	Alboreto	8	9. Lola-Cosworth	3
8	De Cesaris				.	Cheever	8	10. Zakspeed	2
17	Warwick				11.	Nakajima	6	11. Ligier-Megatron	1
18	Cheever					Patrese	6	March-Cosworth	1
9	Brundle				13.	De Cesaris	4		
24	Nannini					Palmer	4		
2	Johansson					Streiff	4		
11	Nakajima				16.	Warwick	3		
10	Danner					Alliot	3		
25	Arnoux				18.	Brundle	2		
23	Campos				19.	Arnoux	1		
16	Capelli					Capelli	1		
26	Ghinzani				**JIM CLARK CUP**			**COLIN CHAPMAN CUP**	
3	Palmer				1.	Palmer	77	1. Tyrrell-Cosworth	145
29	Dalmas				2.	Streiff	68	2. Lola-Cosworth	46
30	Alliot				3.	Alliot	43	3. March-Cosworth	38
4	Streiff				4.	Capelli	38	4. AGS-Cosworth	35
21	Caffi				5.	Fabre	35		
					6.	Dalmas	3		

JAPAN

1st November 1987
Circuit: Suzuka

OUT came the red flag. As Suzuka's first-ever qualifying session for a Japanese Grand Prix came to a halt and the drivers returned to the pit lane in an atmosphere of uneasy calm there came the unwelcome news. 'Nigel's gone off — it looks like a bad one.' In the 120 mph series of bends after the top hairpin Mansell, fighting to regain pole position from his World Championship rival Nelson Piquet, had lost the Williams and gone backwards, very hard indeed, into the tyre wall. Conscious but complaining of back and leg pain he was helicoptered to nearby Nagoya Hospital for treatment prior to a Saturday check by FISA's Doctor, Professor Sid Watkins, to decide whether he would be fit enough for Sunday's crucial race.

Nigel Mansell's last outing of '87 — despite his practice crash and no-start at Suzuka, he has had a superb year.

And when the answer came it was a depressing but absolutely right 'NO'. Nigel was too battered, too bruised and too muscle-strained. Bitterly disappointed he had failed, for the second year in succession, to win the World Championship despite the fact that he had won more races than anyone else. So Nelson Piquet, a very worthy winner of the contest, started the Japanese Grand Prix as World Champion for the third time in his illustrious career — but not, he said, in the way he would ideally have liked.

There had only been two Japanese Grands Prix before and both had been held at the characterless Mount Fuji circuit — in 1976 and '77. Suzuka, though, was much more like it.

Some 35 miles from Nagoya on Honshu Island and owned by Honda it is unique in its layout which takes the form of a severely deformed figure eight with an underpass and flyover at its centre. 3.7 miles long, with two very quick straights and just about every kind of corner including a 60 mph hairpin, it was conceived by the famous racing circuit designer, Dutchman John Hugenholz, and opened in 1962. So Suzuka was celebrating its 25th anniversary and doing so with a fine new pits complex and facilities updated to more than satisfy FISA's severest demands. And for the Motorsport-mad Japanese population their first Grand Prix for ten years was the ultimate lure. So great was the demand for tickets that a nation-wide lottery had to be held to decide who would be able to buy them!

But if this was the 'Big One' for Japan it was by far the biggest one for Honda. In their country's fiercely competitive automotive scene and status-orientated society Suzuka was going to mean more to Honda than all the rest put together. After a brilliant run of success in 1986 and '87 they confidently looked forward to their home race after having seemingly taken over Formula One with twenty wins from the last thirty races — plus sixteen pole positions and twenty-one fastest laps. So as Honda's Racing Boss Yoshitoshi Sakurai contemplated the background and prospects for Sunday's race he was a happy man — the Constructors Championship already crushingly won for Williams-Honda's preference Nelson Piquet the new Drivers World Champion — another Honda win more than likely for, even though Mansell was out, there were still Piquet and Senna to get the job done. And, with Satoru Nakajima at last racing his Lotus-Honda on a GP circuit he knew well, maybe even a 1-2-3 to raise Honda and Japanese prestige yet higher. Life was good! But, as it often does, pride went before a fall.

Honda may have been confident of winning but their desire to do so was no greater than the other top contenders — McLaren, Lotus, Benetton and Ferrari — all of whom wanted nothing more than to beat the Japanese on their home ground. And by two o'clock on Saturday afternoon it amazingly seemed that there was a more than sporting chance of them doing so! Because, for the first time in seventeen races, there was no Honda-powered car on the front row of the grid. Indeed Nelson Piquet, vehemently denying that he was taking it easy now that he'd won the Championship, was only fifth with Honda's other drivers, Senna and Nakajima, seventh and eleventh.

In pole position for the second time in four races, it was Gerhard Berger's sleek-looking, taut-handling and crisp-sounding Ferrari with a time of one minute 40.042 seconds (131.77 mph). And with Alboreto fourth, despite problems, the response that Ferrari's rivals had always feared had at last happened — the Prancing Horse, for so long a spavined travesty of its former self, was rearing again! With Alain Prost second on the grid in his McLaren-TAG ahead of Thierry Boutsen's Benetton-Ford it was four different constructors in the first five places. And right at the back a new boy — Roberto Moreno the experienced, talented and enormously likeable Brazilian driving the AGS in place of Pascal Fabre as a result of the Frenchman's recent inability to qualify.

For no apparent reason the starter seemed to hold the roaring grid for ever. And when he released it Alboreto, with a wildly slipping clutch, stayed where he was whilst those behind miraculously missed him as they surged past. But no such problem for the other Ferrari as Berger blasted into a lead that he did not even lose when he changed his tyres on the 24th of 51 laps. This was the

Nakajima drove a fine race on the circuit he knows best to take sixth place and salvage some pride for Honda.

The start — Berger blasts his way into a lead he never lost — way behind Alliot's Lola is in the pit wall.

occasion that Ferrari and Italy had awaited so long — a dominant, totally convincing win for the Commendatore's men. Just as impressive and as well deserved as the best of the rest during the season and a win that signified with crystal clarity that Ferrari really were back.

But behind Berger, as in Mexico, there was drama in the opening laps. Starting with a fractious shambles at the back caused by the stationary Alboreto that spat Alliot's Lola out of a jostling pack and into the pit-lane armco. And with that sorted out as Berger started his second lap with a staggering lead he was followed not by Prost — as he had been on lap one — but by Boutsen, Senna, Piquet, Fabi and Johansson. Prost was touring back to his pit to change a punctured left rear before restarting, a lap down, to drive a race of pure brilliance that would see him finish almost in the points.

By lap three Berger, intent on breaking the opposition by building a commanding cushion, was six seconds ahead of Boutsen who was similarly out on his own ahead of a superb nose-to-tail scrap for third between Senna, Piquet, Fabi and Johansson followed by the Brabhams of Patrese and De Cesaris — and Nakajima's Lotus.

Even this early in the race it was clear that it was going to be Ferrari's rennaisance day if they went the distance for Alboreto, his clutch now gripping, was racing through the field. As Michele took fifteenth place Johansson slipped past Fabi to fifth whilst Berger made the fastest lap thus far in one minute 49 seconds (120.23 mph). Nine seconds off his pole time but early days yet and with full tanks clearly a lot more still to come. But sadly whilst the Ferraris looked strong, the Benettons did not. Boutsen, with no clutch and too-high fuel

Team Analysis

McLAREN

McLaren balance, power and handling well suited to Suzuka. Prost qualifies second (fastest on Sunday) for only second front-row grid position of 1987. In second place at end of lap one punctures left rear on Alliot start line collision debris. Restarts a lap down after tyre change. Races brilliantly through field to finish seventh, one lap down, with fastest lap (one minute 43.344 secs = 126.210 mph). Johansson ninth on grid. Drives excellent race taking second place after tyre stop and holding it for laps 25-50. Loses second to Senna on last corner as result of being obliged to reduce boost to conserve fuel.

Prost set the fastest lap — after a puncture at the start, he drove brilliantly from last place to seventh.

TYRRELL

After qualifying 19th (second 3½ litre) Palmer drives impressive and trouble-free race to finish excellent eighth overall (one lap down) and win both class and Jim Clark Trophy — thus becoming 'Atmospheric' World Champion. Streiff, beset with loss of power, qualifies lowly 25th and finishes twelfth (two laps down). After very satisfying season Tyrrell now winners of both Jim Clark and Colin Chapman Trophy Championship awards for non-turbo cars.

WILLIAMS

Nigel Mansell destroys race and Championship chances by crashing heavily in Friday qualifying session. With, mercifully, no major injuries resignedly returns to Isle of Man home to rest and recuperate. Piquet qualifies fifth after becoming worthy World Champion for third time. Spends 45 fruitless laps chasing Senna for, at first, second and then third place until engine overheats and destructs as a result of rubber-debris blocked radiators. After long and unrewarding journey to Japan team's substantial consolation is that they have won both Constructors and Drivers Championships.

BRABHAM

Riccardo Patrese, the only driver at Suzuka to have competed in the previous Japanese GP (Fuji 1977) qualifies eighth. Races seventh/eighth for 49 laps. Runs out of fuel, lap 50, but finishes 11th, one lap down. De Cesaris qualifies well at tenth. Improves to eighth but retires lap 27 (engine).

Finishing behind team-mate Palmer meant runner-up position for Philippe Streiff in the 'Atmospheric' Drivers World Championship.

ZAKSPEED

Martin Brundle qualifies satisfactorily at 15th. Retires from 12th (lap 33) with broken engine. Danner sixteenth on grid. Slides harmlessly into armco on own oil, lap 14, after engine blows. Team understood to be running only one car in 1988.

LOTUS

Team well pleased to have both drivers finish in points for third time in 1987. At home circuit Nakajima qualifies eleventh — highest of season. Races strongly — steadily improving from tenth, lap one, to go full distance and take his fourth points-finish in sixth place. Senna qualifies seventh after variety of practice problems. Starts in spare car with 'hot-stuff' Mark Four Honda engine following Sunday warm-up 'Active' suspension trouble with race car. Second laps 12-24 and third after tyre stop — with Piquet ever-present behind rear wing. Takes second place from Johansson (by ³/₁₀ second) on last corner. Now only four points behind second-placed Nigel Mansell in Drivers Championship.

Japan was poignantly disappointing for Williams-Honda — Mansell didn't start and Piquet (here) didn't finish.

AGS

Experienced and immensely capable 28-year-old Brazilian Roberto Moreno replaces too-slow Pascal Fabre as team fights to retain El Charro sponsorship for 1988. In outclassed car Moreno scrapes into race, 26th on grid, as result of injured Mansell non-starting. Races well but retires from first Grand Prix on lap 39 (engine).

MARCH

Capelli 20th on grid (third 3½ litre). Takes class lead in race closely pursued by Jonathan Palmer but retires, lap 14, after collision whilst attempting to pass Arnoux. Team disappointed not to succeed in Leyton House sponsor's home country. Successful pre-Japan tests of Judd V8 engine for 1988 held at Donington and Mauricio Gugelmin confirmed as Team's Number Two driver for next season.

ARROWS

Warwick, with no after-effects from enormous Mexico shunt, qualifies 13th. After poor start due to yellow flag misunderstanding and race marred by gear linkage problems and delayed tyre change caused by too-early Cheever arrival in pit, finishes tenth (one lap down). In qualifying twelfth Cheever blows four engines. In race steadily improves to sixth, lap 48, but runs out of fuel, lap 50. Finishes ninth, one lap down. Team justifiably pleased with another two-car finish.

BENETTON

With traffic problems Fabi (who returns to USA CART racing in 1988) qualifies sixth. Races fifth/sixth for fifteen laps with motor cutting-out before retiring lap 17 (engine). Boutsen, delighted with car's handling and re-mapped engine electronics, starts third. Despite broken clutch holds confident second place, laps 2-11, until need to conserve fuel causes slide to fifth. Push-started after tyre stop. Goes full distance to finish fifth and improve Championship placing to seventh. Team still handicapped by reliability problems.

OSELLA

Caffi starts 23rd. Retires lap 44 (engine). Still no points this season.

MINARDI

Motori-Moderni engine 'Achilles Heel' of Minardi team again causes double-retirement. Campos lap three after qualifying 21st. Nannini lap 36 after starting 14th and then running excellent 11th.

LIGIER

Team arrives at Suzuka with only five Megatron engines for Japanese and Australian Grands Prix. After qualifying seventeenth Arnoux involved with usual 'stock-car' happenings. Drives into Alliot at start whilst avoiding stationary Alboreto. Then, on lap 14, into Capelli as Ivan dives inside to pass. Finally runs out of fuel lap 45. With inadequate practice due to engine shortage Ghinzani starts 24th. Finishes 13th, three laps down, after running dry on last lap.

FERRARI

Forza Ferrari! Success drought ends with pole position and magnificent start-to-finish victory for Berger and fourth place for Alboreto. On well-liked circuit Berger dominates race, including superb 6.97 second tyre stop, to take second-ever win and close within three points of fifth-placed Johansson in Drivers Championship. Alboreto, fourth on grid, badly delayed at start by slipping clutch. Races from 24th to fourth place, including flat-out sixth gear triple spin when shut out by Nannini, in only fourth finish of 1987. With first Ferrari win since 1985 team especially heartened by excellent fuel-consumption achievements.

LOLA

Alliot again qualifies well as top 3½ litre, eighteenth overall. Instant retirement when rammed into pit-lane Armco at start by Alboreto-avoiding Arnoux. Newcomer Yannick Dalmas again impresses in second GP. Starts 22nd and finishes 14th (four laps down) despite sick motor.

For Minardi and Osella 1987 has been hugely disappointing — in Japan they both again failed to score championship points.

Gerhard Berger's second Grand Prix victory was Ferrari's first since 1985 — he totally dominated the race.

consumption, was losing places. Second to Senna. Third to Piquet. And then fourth to Johansson. Three places lost in less than a lap and on lap 17 a disconsolate Teo Fabi rolled into the pit lane and out of the race (engine) with Berger now a very comfortable twelve seconds ahead of the raging battle for second place between Senna and Piquet.

Try as he may Nelson Piquet could make absolutely no impression on his Brazilian countryman's yellow Lotus and to the discomfort, no doubt, of Yoshitoshi Sakurai, glumly standing behind the pit wall, the two Honda

Jim Clark Trophy winner Jonathan Palmer — he clinched the title in Japan.

men, getting in each other's way and slowing each other up, were being caught by Stefan Johansson's McLaren. And Prost was flying too! A new lap record in one minute 47.98 seconds (121.37 mph) as he made up place after place, in a McLaren he later described as 'perfect'.

Johansson was the first to stop for tyres — on lap 21. Into the pits in fourth place, out in sixth behind Berger, Senna, Piquet, Boutsen and Alboreto. Alboreto? Yes! For Michele was now a stunning fifth. And, as ever, things were raging in the 'Atmospheric' class. Capelli, leading Jonathan Palmer, had retired on lap 16 to let the Doctor take control of the 3½ litre category. If he stayed ahead of his Tyrrell team-mate Philippe Streiff, Jonathan would win the Jim Clark Trophy and effectively become the class World Champion. Which gloriously he did.

When the leaders had all stopped for tyres (with Boutsen being push-started and the Ferrari pit crew taking a mere 6.97 seconds to change Berger's four wheels and tyres) it was Gerhard still serenely ahead. But now Johansson was an excellent second ahead of the battling Senna and Piquet who had made their tyre stops together — a stirring sight! Lap 34 — a record for Berger in one minute 45.54 seconds (124.18 mph) which was immediately broken by Prost (1.45.13). And although the crowd's attention was rivetted on the first four they should have spared a glance for Alain who was now only sixty seconds behind the sixth place man Satoru Nakajima, and driving at incredible speed with the smooth precision that has twice made him World Champion.

All the time Nelson Piquet, conscious of his newly-gained World Champion status, lectured by Honda before the race about how important it was for them to win and angered by the fact that the man ahead of him was his bitter rival Ayrton Senna, had been right behind the Lotus-Honda. Which was his undoing. On lap 46, as rubber debris filled his radiators, and with smoke billowing out behind his Williams he slowly drew up to his pit, unbuckled his safety belt and got out to retire. Whilst millions of fascinated TV viewers all over the world watched a jet of black oil vigorously pumping out of his engine on to Suzuka's pristine surface. Honda's misery was complete.

Gerhard Berger brilliantly and deservedly won the Japanese Grand Prix by 17½ seconds with Michele Alboreto an excellent fourth after a fighting come-back from 24th place on lap one in a reliable Ferrari — a fine drive marred only by his fluffed start. But for that he could well have been second. What a turn round for Maranello! Ahead of Alboreto Stefan Johansson had led them all except Berger for 26 laps and for a time was within two seconds of the leading Ferrari. But in the closing stages he had to turn down his turbo boost to conserve fuel — and that gave Senna his chance. To a roar from the crowd Ayrton took Johansson and second place as they exited the last corner!

So with Senna second and Nakajima sixth Honda, by their demanding standards, had massively lost face in a day of comparative failure. But that's racing. It was Honda's misfortune that they lost the one that mattered most.

But with the glory of a Ferrari win, a new World Champion, Palmer finishing eighth and winning the Jim Clark Trophy and Prost coming home a superb seventh with the fastest lap of the day 126.210 mph the Japanese Grand Prix had been one to remember. As a postcript Gerhard Berger generously paid tribute to the absent Nigel Mansell after his epic victory. 'I'd never been to Suzuka before but I realised that Nigel knew the place from his test sessions for Honda so I asked him to show me the way round. You'd expect him to keep things to himself but he didn't. He showed me the best lines on every corner and when I tried them they were right. It was nice of him to do that.' I'll say it was! But the way Gerhard went at Suzuka I doubt that even Nigel could have beaten him. It would have been nice to see him try though . . .

In full view of millions of TV viewers, Nelson Piquet's great efforts in Japan ended in the pits, his Honda engine spewing oil 'on to the pristine Suzuka pit lane'.

Nelson Piquet's deserving army of fans going 'overboard' at his championship success.

JAPANESE GRAND PRIX

Winner: Gerhard Berger, Ferrari F187/097   *Fastest Lap:* Alain Prost, 126.210 mph

GRID POSITION			RESULTS		
No.		Driver	Pos.	Driver	Car
	28	Berger	1	Berger	Ferrari F187/097
1		Prost	2	Senna	Lotus-Honda 99T/6
	20	Boutsen	3	Johansson	McLaren-TAG MP4/3-5
27		Alboreto	4	Alboreto	Ferrari F187/101
	6	Piquet	5	Boutsen	Benetton-Ford B187-09
19		Fabi	6	Nakajima	Lotus-Honda 99T/3
	12	Senna	7	Prost	McLaren-TAG MP4/3-4
7		Patrese	8	Palmer	Tyrrell Cosworth DG/016-5
	2	Johansson	9	Cheever	Arrows-Megatron A10/2
8		De Cesaris	10	Warwick	Arrows-Megatron A10/4
	11	Nakajima	11	Patrese	Brabham-BMW BT56/4
18		Cheever	12	Streiff	Tyrrell-Cosworth DG/016-2
	17	Warwick			
24		Nannini			
	9	Brundle			
10		Danner			
	25	Arnoux			
30		Alliot			
	3	Palmer			
16		Capelli			
	23	Campos			
29		Dalmas			
	21	Caffi			
26		Ghinzani			
	4	Streiff			
14		Moreno			

WORLD CHAMPIONSHIP

Drivers		Pts	Constructors		Pts
1.	Piquet	73	1.	Williams-Honda	137
2.	Mansell	61	2.	McLaren-TAG	76
3.	Senna	57	3.	Lotus-Honda	64
4.	Prost	46	4.	Ferrari	38
5.	Johansson	30	5.	Benetton-Ford	24
6.	Berger	27	6.	Arrows-Megatron	11
7.	Boutsen	12	7.	Brabham-BMW	10
	Fabi	12	8.	Tyrrell-Cosworth	8
9.	Alboreto	11	9.	Lola-Cosworth	3
10.	Cheever	8	10.	Zakspeed	2
11.	Nakajima	7	11.	Ligier-Megatron	1
12.	Patrese	6		March-Cosworth	1
13.	De Cesaris	4			
	Palmer	4			
	Streiff	4			
16.	Alliot	3			
	Warwick	3			
18.	Brundle	2			
19.	Arnoux	1			
	Capelli	1			

JIM CLARK CUP			COLIN CHAPMAN CUP		
1.	Palmer	86	1.	Tyrrell-Cosworth	160
2.	Streiff	74	2.	Lola-Cosworth	50
3.	Alliot	43	3.	March-Cosworth	38
4.	Capelli	38	4.	AGS-Cosworth	35
5.	Fabre	35			
6.	Dalmas	7			

AUSTRALIA

15th November 1987
Circuit: Adelaide

AND so to what is generally regarded in the Grand Prix world as being the climax of the season — the Australian Grand Prix. And not just because it is the last of the sixteen-race series. But because Adelaide is special.

The Australian Grand Prix has a long history. It was first held in 1928 and has catered for a variety of formulae. Immediately prior to 1985 it existed for what Europeans used to call Formula Two cars but for years there had been efforts to hold a 'proper' Formula One World Championship race 'down under'. The rivalry between the competing cities to win the approval of FOCA's Bernie Ecclestone was intense. Sydney evolved a course in the 'Rocks' area within sight of the Opera House and its world-famous 'Coathanger' bridge. Melbourne had plans too. But Adelaide, the city that many Australians dismissively refer to as 'Sleepy Hollow', to general amazement, won the day, largely thanks to the personal initiative and enterprise of South Australia's Premier John Bannon.

And when we arrived there in 1985, totally ignorant of what to expect, how enchanted we were! A delightful city not far from the home of some of Australia's finest wines, the appropriately named McLaren Vale, and a charming, cheerful and energetic populace whose hospitality and enthusiasm for Grand Prix racing knew no bounds. For years seemingly half of Australia had got up in the small hours of the morning excitedly to watch the whole of every Grand Prix live on television. Now it was actually here and they were going to make the most of it!

And to do so they'd produced a magnificent circuit. Not a purpose-built artificial track like most of the rest but a street circuit that was, in the words of Martin Brundle, 'like Monaco without the buildings'. That may sound an odd way to describe it but it is very apt for Adelaide's 2.35 miles, 105 mph lap, comprising everyday roads and streets on the outskirts

of the city which pass the fruit market, pubs and houses, cross open parkland and, via a specially constructed section, traverse the historic Victoria Park Racecourse.

And no expense had been spared to produce the best possible facilities. Superb pits garages which even included their own engineering workshop. Magnificent grand-

Turn again Michele — this practice spin didn't stop Alboreto scoring an excellent race 2nd place — some consolation for a frustrating season.

stands and hospitality suites. Television coverage which won the FOCA award in 1985 and '86. Australia had sent representatives from every area of activity to the world's Grands Prix to see how it was done and they'd equalled or exceeded the best.

And the racing matched the scene. Victory for Keke Rosberg's Williams-Honda at the inaugural 1985 race. The World Championship dramatically decided in favour of Alain Prost in 1986 when, in the closing stages of the race, Nigel Mansell had imminent success snatched from his hands by an exploding left rear tyre.

The drivers liked the circuit. The teams loved the facilities and the atmosphere. The enormous crowd and the Australian nation were enraptured. This was a new jewel in Grand Prix racing's crown.

But without the charisma of 'First Time '85' and 'Championship-decider '86' was 1987 going to be anti-climactic? Just another Grand Prix on the other side of the world for the tired teams to play out the end of the season? Not a bit of it! For not only was it Adelaide, Australia — in itself an exciting and stimulating experience — but this was going to be the scene of many 'last appearances'. With all the teams and drivers out to prove something.

The last Grand Prix for turbocars with 4 bar boost and 195 litres of fuel. McLaren's last race with TAG engines after four years of enormous success. Williams' last race with Honda after similar outstanding achievement. March's last race with Cosworth power, and Ligier's with Megatron motors. The 1987 World Champion Nelson Piquet's last race with Williams, Ayrton Senna's with Lotus. Fabi's with Benetton, Johansson's with McLaren, and, for all we knew at the time, his sad total departure from Grand Prix racing. And, doubtless, many other 'lasts' that were still secret. But, to everyone's deep regret, we'd already seen one of the most notable final appearances of all — that of Nigel Mansell with the car-engine combination with which he had won 13 Grands Prix in the last three seasons. Still recovering from his violent battering in Japan, Nigel wasn't even in Australia — which meant that not only had he had his last Honda-powered drive in a Williams but that he would be unable to take up his invitation to compete in the Australian Open Golf Championship.

So, except for Mansell's absence, there was plenty to look forward to when practising started on 13th November!

Adelaide had fought hard in 1985 to stage the post-war World Championship Grand Prix. In 1987 they celebrated the third anniversary of their famous victory by staging what was, quite simply, the best race of the year in an atmosphere of joyful enthusiasm which more than lifted the spirits of the travel-weary Grand Prix regulars.

The weather in 1985 had been suspect. In 1986 surprised visitors discovered that it rained in Australia — seemingly non-stop although the race was dry — but 1987 was glorious. Clear blue skies, blazing sunshine

building to 40° heat on race day and a sparkingly clear atmosphere that was a photographer's delight.

Two men dominated the two days of practice — Gerhard Berger and Alain Prost — each of whom topped the list twice. But significantly it was the Austrian in his Ferrari who not only took pole position for the second race in succession but who also headed the time sheet for Sunday's 'in-race-trim' final half hour. With Prost second on the grid, Piquet third (in a standard-suspension Williams although he had also used an 'Active' car built up with parts flown out at his special request), Senna fourth, Boutsen fifth and Alboreto sixth there were no surprises at the front. But further back there were two new situations — Riccardo Patrese seventh in a William-Honda and Stefano Modena an astonishing fifteenth in a Brabham-BMW. Both were the result of

Proving there is smoke without fire — Michele Alboreto

Nigel Mansell's absence — Patrese had been released from the Brabham team to start his Williams career a race early whilst 24-year-old Modena, the European Formula 3000 Champion of 1987, took Patrese's Brabham place as a welcome but totally unexpected extra prize for his F3000 success. He astounded and delighted everyone with his skill and maturity and showed himself to be a Grand Prix star of the future.

It was going to be a long, hard and very demanding race. The heat, the twists and turns of Adelaide for nearly the maximum permissible two hours and prospects of no stops for tyres were not only going to put a premium on car and driver fitness but were

Dalmas — fifth place in only his
third Grand Prix.

going to give the 3½ litre cars a chance to
shine. And they did!

At 14.00 on Sunday, 15th November, the
lights turned to green and Piquet blasted into
the lead from row two of the grid. But only for
a few hundred metres as, with stunning ease,
Berger sliced past the Williams into the first
place that was to remain his for 82 non-stop
laps. All the drivers later agreed that Adelaide

was the toughest race of the year but Berger
— very ably supported by Alboreto — devasta-
tingly showed that both he and Ferrari had got
the stamina and speed to stay at the front and
this despite a virus infection!

Close behind him though there was a
marvellous fight which captivated the sun-
baked 123,000 crowd (250,000 attended the
four day meeting) as, for 34 laps, Piquet, Prost,

At the edge — Berger on his way to victory, Prost on his way to the tyre-wall and retirement.

Team Analysis

McLAREN

Disappointing last race with TAG engine. Prost qualifies second fastest despite back pain caused by Friday spin. Down to fourth lap one. Races with Piquet/Senna/Alboreto, to second lap 35. Back to fourth lap 42 before spinning harmlessly into tyre wall and retirement, lap 54 (broken brake disc). Ends season 4th in World Championship. Johansson, in last race for McLaren, starts eighth. Progress to fifth by lap 35 only to retire, lap 49, also with broken brake disc. 6th in World Championship but uncertain future for 1988. Team second in Constructors Championship, prepares for 1988 with Honda engine.

TYRRELL

Excellent finish for 1988 with team winning both 3½ litre Championships after eleven class victories and achieving target of eleven main championship points. After starting 19th and sliding to 23rd with puncture Palmer brilliantly takes highest-of-season 4th place, winning class for seventh time. Wins Jim Clark Trophy and finishes top 'Atmospheric' driver at eleventh equal in overall Championship. Streiff qualifies 18th and retires, lap seven (puncture and suspension), finishes second in Jim Clark Trophy contest, Tyrrell excellent sixth-equal in overall Constructors Championship.

WILLIAMS

Team finishes superb double-championship season (Drivers and Constructors) on dull note at last race with Honda-power. In final GP Williams new World Champion Piquet

'No it's not Nigel, it's Riccardo'. Patrese's first and last drive for Williams-Honda ended in ninth place.

qualifies third after using both 'Active' and standard suspension cars. In standard car second to Berger laps 1-34. Down to sixth, lap 35, after tyre stop. Recovers to fourth but retires, lap 59, (broken gearchange and brake disc). In superb season with three wins and seven second places Piquet equals Alain Prost highest, with 76 Championship points. Riccardo Patrese released early by Brabham to replace absent Mansell in second car. Qualifies seventh. Holds fourth place laps 62-76 but retires lap 77 after consuming all engine oil.

BRABHAM

1987 European Formula 3000 Champion Stefano Modena brilliantly substitutes for Riccardo Patrese. Qualifies outstanding fifteenth (staggering fifth fastest in Saturday warm-up!). Twelfth place by lap 3 but after stopping for three sets of tyres (wheelspin) retires from first GP, lap 32, overcome by fatigue. De Cesaris starts tenth. Retires from eleventh, lap 36, (electrics) after last race with BMW engines. Team's GP future uncertain.

ZAKSPEED

In, possibly, last race with team Brundle qualifies 16th. Progresses to twelfth but retires lap 19. (Stuck in second with broken gear lever so turbo over-speeds and breaks). Danner starts 24th after Saturday practice time disallowed due to empty fire extinguisher. Races well to finish seventh (three laps down) in spite of 'no brakes'.

LOTUS

Unhappy end to long trip. Street circuit-hater Nakajima qualifies 14th. Retires lap 23 (Active-suspension oil leak). In last race after three seasons and six wins with Lotus, Senna starts fourth. Opportunistically passes Alboreto and Prost to second lap 42. Halves gap to Berger to eight seconds after repeatedly breaking lap record. With worn tyres abandons chase to finish worthy second but, following Benetton protest disqualified for 'unlawful body dimensions due to oversize brake ducting'. As a result of this fails to equal Mansell second-place Drivers Championship score and remains third. Team finish season third in Constructors Team Championship.

AGS

Unexpected windfall results in team's best race of season. Roberto Moreno, in second GP, starts 25th. By steadily plugging away finishes excellent seventh in outclassed car (three laps down) which becomes sixth after Senna disqualification. This earns team single Championship point which will drastically reduce their 1988 travel costs.

MARCH

In last race with Cosworth-power 'Dustin Hoffman'-lookalike Ivan Capelli qualifies 23rd. In excellent drive leads 3½ litre class and achieves excellent seventh place on lap 54 only to spin out of contention, lap 59, when car loses downforce cornering behind Berger Ferrari. Team now prepares for two-car 1988 Championship assault with 3½ litre 'Atmospheric' Judd engines.

The last time for Nelson Piquet in a Williams — the race sponsor's product clearly 'reached his parts' — his gearshift broke!

Stefano Modena — Grand Prix debutant.

ARROWS

For seventh successive race Warwick and Cheever occupy same starting grid row — Cheever 11th and Warwick 12th. Both fail to finish. Warwick out lap 20 when eleventh (gearbox seal). Cheever out lap 54 (overheating engine) after running ninth laps 10-47. Team finish creditable sixth-equal (with Tyrrell) in Constructors Championship.

BENETTON

In his last race with the team Teo Fabi starts from 9th on grid. Races 10th/11th for twenty-five laps before multiple tyre-changes (wheelspin) and failing brakes lead to lap 47 retirement from 14th place (last but three). From fifth on grid Boutsen has usual impressive drive to finish fourth when becomes third following Senna disqualification. Team finish disappointing fifth in Constructors Championship after failing to realise potential as a result of a series of development problems.

OSELLA

Talented Caffi again fails to qualify.

MINARDI

Team thankfully race for the last time with fragile Motori Moderni engine before switching to Cosworth power for 1988. Another disheartening meeting after both drivers fail to finish. Campos writes off car in practice before qualifying 26th in spare. Retires from 17th and last place, lap 47, with broken gearbox. Nannini qualifies well at 13th but retires from race immediately after start by hitting concrete barrier on exit of first corner.

LIGIER

With usual limited Megatron engine supply Arnoux qualifies 26th and Ghinzani 22nd. After running 10th for laps 15-41 Arnoux retires lap 42 (camshaft). Ghinzani races at tail of field with electrical pick-up problem until lap 27 retirement. After miserable season due to first Alfa-Romeo and then Megatron engine problems, Ligier thankfully turn to development of all-new 1988 car with 3½ litre Judd 'Atmospheric' engine.

FERRARI

Superb end-of-season race brilliantly completes Ferrari revival with first 1-2 finish for team since Canada 1985. Berger dominates practice to take second successive pole position (and third in five successive races), before equally dominating race after leading all 82 laps wins by over a minute at record speed and with record lap of 1.20.416 (105.735 mph), advances one place to fifth in Drivers World Championship. Alboreto qualifies 6th after traffic problems. Fifth, laps 1-4. Fourth, laps 5-34. Third, laps 35-82 with brake problems. Third becomes second after Senna disqualification. Improves two places in Drivers Championship (to 7th). Team finishes fourth in Constructors Championship with very high morale and now faces 1988 with renewed enthusiasm.

LOLA

Curates Egg race for Gerard Larrousse's team. Talented Yannick Dalmas starts 21st and races to excellent fifth place in race (though points not counted as too few races). Alliot again qualifies as fastest 3½ litre (17th) but retires from same position, lap 46, (electronics). In first Grand Prix year Team finishes ninth in main Constructors Championship and second to Tyrrell in 'Atmospheric' category.

'And I'll lead you through the streets of Adelaide' Senna heads Berger in practice — their roles were reversed in the race.

Superstitious Stefano Modena — his inside-out driving glove being only one of his little idiosyncrasies — a very fine first drive nevertheless.

Alboreto and Senna raced practically nose to tail. It is very hard to pass at Adelaide but there was certainly no lack of effort to do so!

Patrese was sixth in his first race for Williams until lap 25 when Johansson, with the then fastest lap (1:23.4) moved into the points with Boutsen eighth.

But such was the pressure up front that Prost made a rare mistake by leaping across the chicane kerbing on lap 28 — a mistake which brought Alboreto (fourth) and Senna even closer to the McLaren-TAG. Then, with the fuel loads decreasing, a string of new fastest laps from Berger, Alboreto, Johansson, Prost and Senna. Fuel consumption was a problem for all of them but it certainly didn't look like it.

On lap 34 1987 World Champion Nelson Piquet lost his chance to end the season with the highest-ever points total — and to enable Williams to do the same in the Constructors

Making his point — Roberto Moreno's sixth place was a great reward for the AGS team.

Championship. Some were able to preserve their tyres but he wasn't and when he rejoined the race after a pit stop, he was down to sixth behind the meteoric Berger, Prost, Alboreto, Senna and Johansson. And destined not to last much longer.

But now Prost was on his challenging way with a new fastest lap in 1:22.179 (102.86 mph). Berger was leading by 13 seconds but at just over half distance, lap 42, the street-fighters behind him — Prost, Alboreto and Senna — almost instantaneously changed places as they lapped René Arnoux (Ligier) and Christian Danner (Zakspeed) who were squabbling for tenth place. Senna up to second, Alboreto up to third and Prost down to fourth in just a few

Eddie Cheever's Arrows quivers — an overheating engine stopped him on lap 54.

metres! And Berger, with a clear track ahead of him was now 18 seconds ahead of them and looking totally relaxed.

We'd seen some stirring drives in 1987 but there now began one of the very best as Ayrton Senna, scenting a possible win in his last drive for Lotus, set about catching the Ferrari ahead. Lap 47 — a new lap record. 1:20.73 = 104.71 mph. And the gap slowly started to close as Stefan Johansson lost his fifth place in what may have been his last Grand Prix when a brake disc exploded. Lap 52 — another Senna record: 1:20.63 = 104.846 mph as Prost slammed out of fourth place and harmlessly into the tyre wall with, like his team mate Johansson, an exploded brake disc. Everyone had known that Adelaide was going to be hard on brakes and it was living up to its destructive reputation.

So, on lap 54, Berger led Senna (by only eight seconds now) with Alboreto a confident third in his crisp-sounding Ferrari, Piquet up

Close examination of Ayrton Senna's nearside wheel shows the illegal brake cooling ducts which resulted in his disqualification.

to fourth, Boutsen to fifth, Patrese to sixth and the lapped Ivan Capelli an excellent seventh — leading the 3½ litre category from Palmer, Dalmas and Moreno.

Only 12 of the 26 starters were left on lap 55 when Berger responded to a radio warning from his pit that Senna was closing. With sparks flying as part of his Ferrari bodywork grounded on the bumps he put in a series of electrifying record laps which destroyed Senna's challenge — culminating with the fastest of the day (1:20.46 = 105.735) on lap 72. As he did so Piquet followed up his 'damp squib' Japanese drive with another by retiring with a broken gearshift and a shattered brake disc, leaving only Berger, Senna and Alboreto on the same lap and therefore well ahead of Boutsen (fourth), Patrese and Palmer. Jonathan was now a magnificent sixth having fought his way up from practically last after a lap eight puncture.

But Palmer was to improve again! Firstly to fifth when Patrese sadly parked his oil-less Williams-Honda on lap 62 and then to fourth (his best of the year) after the race had finished.

After the race had finished? Yes, because after Berger, Senna and Alboreto had deservedly received an ecstatic reception from the massive crowd and given their TV interviews it was announced that the unfortunate Senna had been excluded as the result of a successful protest from the Benetton team that his specially-fitted brake cooling ducts

offended the bodywork regulations. Tough? Certainly. But in the weary words of Senna, robbed of the reward of a fine drive, 'that's motor racing'.

So, apart from that sour event, 1987 ended on an enormous high with the Ferraris of Berger and Alboreto achieving Maranello's first 1-2 since Canada 1985. Boutsen's Benetton was the only other turbo car in the top six for with Palmer's Tyrrell fourth, Dalmas's Lola fifth (in only his third GP) and Moreno giving the hard-trying little French AGS team its first World Championship point it was 3½ litre cars that filled the remaining top places.

A great end to a great season and a sign that, with the regulations changing in favour of the 'atmospheric' cars, we could look forward to an even more closely-contested 1988.

Stefan in the shade — not for long we hope.

Thanks for the memories — 1987 was a superb year for Grand Prix motor racing.

AUSTRALIAN GRAND PRIX

Winner: Gerhard Berger, Ferrari F187/097   *Fastest Lap:* Gerhard Berger, 105.734 mph

GRID POSITION		RESULTS			WORLD CHAMPIONSHIP			
No.	Driver	Pos.	Driver	Car	Drivers	Pts	Constructors	Pts
28	Berger	1	Berger	Ferrari F187-097	1. Piquet	73	1. Williams-Honda	137
1	Prost	2	Alboreto	Ferrari F187-101	2. Mansell	61	2. McLaren-TAG	76
6	Piquet	3	Boutsen	Benetton-Ford B187-09	3. Senna	57	3. Lotus-Honda	64
12	Senna	4	Palmer	Tyrrell-Cosworth DG/016-2	4. Prost	46	4. Ferrari	53
20	Boutsen	5	Dalmas	Lola-Cosworth LC87/02	5. Berger	36	5. Benetton-Ford	28
27	Alboreto	6	Moreno	AGS-Cosworth JH22/02	6. Johansson	30	6. Arrows-Megatron	11
5	Patrese	7	Danner	Zakspeed 871/02	7. Alboreto	17	Tyrrell-Cosworth	11
2	Johansson	8	De Cesaris	Brabham-BMW BT56/2	8. Boutsen	16	8. Brabham-BMW	10
19	Fabi	9	Patrese	Williams-Honda FW11B/1	9. Fabi	12	9. Lola-Cosworth	3
8	De Cesaris				10. Cheever	8	10. Zakspeed	2
18	Cheever				11. Nakajima	7	11. AGS-Cosworth	1
17	Warwick				Palmer	7	Ligier-Megatron	1
24	Nannini				13. Patrese	6	March-Cosworth	1
11	Nakajima				14. De Cesaris	4		
7	Modena				Streiff	4		
9	Brundle				16. Alliot	3		
30	Alliot				Warwick	3		
4	Streiff				18. Brundle	2		
3	Palmer				19. Arnoux	1		
25	Arnoux				Capelli	1		
29	Dalmas				Moreno	1		
26	Ghinzani							
16	Capelli				**JIM CLARK CUP**		**COLIN CHAPMAN CUP**	
10	Danner				1. Palmer	95	1. Tyrrell-Cosworth	169
14	Moreno				2. Streiff	74	2. Lola-Cosworth	56
23	Campos				3. Alliot	43	3. AGS-Cosworth	39
					4. Capelli	38	4. March-Cosworth	38
					5. Fabre	35		
					6. Dalmas	13		
					7. Moreno	4		

REVIEW OF 1987 — A VINTAGE YEAR!

In looking back at the 1987 season so soon after it has finished and with the memories of Australia still at the top of my mind it is not easy to put the season as a whole into perspective. But whatever your yardstick for measurement there is no doubt that the year of 1987 has been one of great worldwide achievement for Formula One. Sixteen enormously successful World Championship races held in fifteen countries (I cannot, in all conscience, call the San Marino GP anything other than Italian!). Hundreds of thousands of people paid big money (some would say too big) to go and see them and hundreds of millions more all over the world turned on and tuned in their TV sets to watch and listen to the gladiatorial action — and become hooked on it.

That's because Grand Prix racing has a unique appeal. Not just the colour, the noise, the speed and the danger but the fact that, unlike most other sports, it is a combination of man and machine. The best driver in the world will never succeed without the right car any more than a poor driver can win in the best car. So taking both elements — man and machine — into account what were the high spots of 1987?

First and foremost, in my view, the domination of the Williams team — their cars, drivers, designers, technicians, mechanics and back-up personnel at their Didcot base. Their second successive Constructors Championship (and their fourth since 1980) plus first and second places in the Drivers Championship is a glowing tribute to them all — and in particular to Frank Williams and Patrick Head. Together, as Team Principal and Designer, they have created a unique and long-lasting partnership and their 1987 success is not only a more than well deserved reward for both of them but a stirring tribute to the supreme courage and determination of Frank in overcoming the crippling effects of his devastating 1986 road crash. At the end of 1985 I remember thinking 'will anyone ever beat McLaren?' Well Williams have and not just once but twice in a row.

For McLaren 1987 was, by their supremely high standards, a poor year. Because for them finishing second is not good enough. To what extent this was because of the departure of their brilliant designer John Barnard, the man who drew and developed the enormously successful MP4, only they can say — and I don't suppose they would! However, the unexpected unreliability of their TAG engine, previously one of the team's strongest points, severely depressed their race performances and achievements.

In a sport which is seldom short of sensation and speculation 1987 saw a major move which shook everyone and which, to many, seemed inexplicable — the defection of Honda from Williams to McLaren for 1988. The truth of the matter is that it just isn't possible to judge Japanese action by Western standards. What, on the face of it, seems to be an astonishing act of ingratitude and disloyalty is apparently a perfectly logical business-oriented move to the Japanese. The whole issue has been clouded by the fact that Honda have never really come out into the open and fully explained their motives. Nor have Williams. But whatever the motivation, the result is likely to be that the positions of Williams and McLaren are reversed in 1988 — McLaren will be Honda powered and their drivers will be Prost and Senna — an awesome combination. Williams, on the other hand, will have lost 1987 World Champion Nelson Piquet and will be powered by the new and unproven 'Atmospheric' Judd engine.

To me one of the most heartening and satisfying things about the 1987 season was the resurgence of Ferrari. It had been a sad and embarrassing sight to see the mighty Italian concern, winner of more Grands Prix than any other constructor and the team for which so many of motor racing's immortals had driven, floundering about amongst the also-rans for over two years. The Commendatore's decision to recruit John Barnard to technically-mastermind his team back to the top was indeed a brave one for it caused bitter dissension amongst the ranks at Maranello. But whilst Barnard got his head down in Guildford to design a Ferrari winner for 1988, his English compatriot Dr Harvey Postlethwaite was beavering away in Italy to save the

1987 day. Berger's second place on the grid in Hungary and his subsequent pole position in Portugal were the first heartening signs that he was well on the road to doing so. By spending endless hours in the new wind tunnel at Maranello perfecting the 187's aerodynamics and achieving an effective suspension set-up Harvey transformed the car's handling. With increased, if not always reliable engine power Ferrari were on the pace and Berger's superb victory in Japan, the

A wonderful year for Ken Tyrrell — 'Atmospheric' constructors trophy for his team, and 3½ litre drivers title for Jonathan Palmer.

team's first since Germany 1985, gave them back their self-respect and the acclamation of everyone who cares for the great Italian team's place in Grand Prix racing. So now it is up to John Barnard to show that his endeavours will continue the Ferrari revival in 1988.

1987 was notable for three other major technical achievements — 'Active' Suspension, Pop-Off valves and Goodyear tyres. It was courageous of Lotus to turn their backs on conventional suspension and concentrate 100% on their innovative new system — a

move which, whilst not entirely successful i 1987, gave them an enormous amount oi race-experience which will have shot them right up the learning curve for 1988. The fact that the Williams team raced their much-tested simpler system at Monza, Portugal and Spain showed that this is the way everyone will have to go — ignoring the emotional President of FISA's statement that he intends to ban their use in 1988!

Pop-Off valves were one of the success stories of 1987. Introduced by the much-maligned FISA (Governing Body of Motor Sport) amidst prophesies of failure, broken engines and frustrated drivers they proved to be well-nigh faultless in achieving their objective of limiting turbo boost to 4.0 bar. Well done FISA! And well done Goodyear too. When Pirelli pulled out of Formula One at the end of 1986 Goodyear sportingly, and at vast expense, undertook to carry the whole of the load. It is no exaggeration to say that withou them Grand Prix racing would have been chaotic shambles in 1987 and would certainly have ceased to exist in its present impressive form. The Sport owes an enormous debt of gratitude to Goodyear.

Was it wise to have a dual-formula in 1987 with 850 horsepower turbocars racing against the 550 horsepower 'atmospherics'? The answer depends on who you are talking to. But if you believe, as I do, that FISA's decision to ban turbos after 1988 was laudable it must be 'yes'. Without the availability of the lower-cost Cosworth engine it is doubtful whether the Tyrrell, March, Lola and AGS teams would have been able to compete in 1987 and they

'Look at it my way Bernie'. 'No! Look at it mine Jean-Marie.' Together Ecclestone and Balestre run Grand Prix racing.

rtainly gave us some stimulating racing to watch — if you could wrench your eyes away from what was happening at the front!

In a year of exciting and memorable competition the following Grand Prix will live in my memory. Significantly most of them featured Nigel Mansell in a leading role. Belgium where he undeniably blotted his copy-book by assaulting Senna after their on-track confrontation. Monaco where he retired from a commanding lead to enable Ayrton Senna to create history by becoming the first man to win a Grand Prix in an 'Actively' suspended car. Silverstone where Nigel brought a patriotic lump to millions of British throats by inspiredly catching, and then passing his team-mate Nelson Piquet on his way to his second successive home GP victory. Germany, where Alain Prost was cruelly robbed of a record breaking 28th Grand Prix win and where 3½ litre cars, totally against expectations, finished fourth, fifth and sixth. Austria where Mansell inadvertently caused the second of the multi-car start-line pile-ups. Portugal where Prost finally became the most successful Grand Prix driver of all time by masterfully taking that elusive 28th World Championship win — and where Ferrari really started to show their teeth. Spain where Mansell brilliantly and grimly dominated a breathtakingly exciting race almost from the green light to the chequered flag, won his fifth Grand Prix of the year and kept alive his slim hopes of winning the World Championship. And finally, Japan, where Mansell sadly missed the race after his practice crash, and where Nelson Piquet became a very worthy third-time World Champion.

Another well deserved accolade to FISA too for laying down and implementing the exacting safety standards to which today's GP cars are built — and to their designers for meeting them so successfully. Six men undoubtedly owe their lives to them — Nelson Piquet at Imola, Jonathan Palmer and Philippe Streiff in Belgium and Monaco, Stefan Johansson who was able to practise in another car shortly after hitting that unfortunate deer in Austria. Derek Warwick who safely survived enormous impact in Mexico. And Nigel Mansell, who may have failed to compete in Japan as a result of his practice crash but who mercifully suffered nothing worse than aches and bruises.

Images of a brilliant triple World Champion.

Ready

Steady

Go!

143

hitting that unfortunate deer in Austria. Derek Warwick who safely survived enormous impact in Mexico. And Nigel Mansell, who may have failed to compete in Japan as a result of his practice crash but who mercifully suffered nothing worse than aches and bruises.

Grand Prix racing is about cars, about circuits, about politics, money and teamwork. But it is the drivers who people talk about the most. So, to end an all too brief review of the Year of '87 who have been, and are, the best? The answer to that question, too, depends on who you are talking to and what your yardsticks are. With his superb third World Championship, achieved with a record equalling 73 points from three wins, seven seconds and one third, Nelson Piquet was, of course, the most successful driver of 1987. It was sad that, in Japan, he became Champion by default, as a result of Mansell's practice crash but his success is no less worthy because of that. So Piquet takes the coveted 'Number One' to Lotus for 1988 and richly deserves the honour. But is he the best? To be World Champion you have to be the right man in the right car — and to have the luck run your way. Piquet satisfied all those requirements. But Mansell will be able gloomily to reflect that in an outstanding season of personal achievement, and as in 1986, he won more races than anyone else and was in a potentially race-winning situation on three other occasions when he had to retire through no fault of his. For Alain Prost, too, it was an unprecedented succession of engine problems that depressed his achievements rather than any fading of his brilliant talent. Whilst, in my opinion, there is little, if anything, to choose between Piquet, Prost and Mansell if I was obliged to rank them in terms of driving talent as opposed to 1987 success I'd do so, amidst angry protestations no doubt, in the order of Prost, Mansell and Piquet.

For those who agree with me no justification is needed. To those who do not I would say, whilst you are entitled to your own opinion, consider these points. Prost's amazing run of World Championship successes since he first drove for McLaren in 1980, his record number of wins, his uncanny ability always to be at the front when it matters, his tactical skill and his effortless, smooth and flowing style prove that he is currently in a class of his own. To put Mansell in second place ahead of Piquet was, for me, not difficult. For the last two years he has consistently out-qualified and out-driven his Brazilian team-mate, has demonstrated the most impressive consistency and ability to resist the most extreme pressure and, but for his appalling luck would have dominated 1987 in a way seldom seen before.

Piquet ahead of Senna? Yes but this year Piquet had the better car and it will be more than interesting to see how they compare with each other in their new teams during 1988. Senna's brilliance was regrettably masked this year by a car which, good as the Lotus is, did not allow him to exploit his outstanding talent to the full. And, finally, more than honourable mentions for Thierry Boutsen, Michele Alboreto, Gerhard Berger and Jonathan Palmer, four men who, like Senna, were too often inhibited by their cars from fully demonstrating their considerable talents. Their time will come. Hopefully in 1988, for Grand Prix racing needs different names in different cars at the front if it is not to become boring to the TV masses on whom it ultimately depends.

With the exciting prospects for 1988 that are before us — closer racing between the turbo and atmospheric cars, ever more impressive technical developments, driver changes, new engines and a great World Champion back at the top to defend his place on the pinnacle of Motor Racing achievement the coming season will doubtless be as rewarding for enthusiasts and viewers as the last. Here's to it!